From

Boroughmuir

to

Branxton Moor

The Story of Flodden

James Douglas Bell

Published in 2004
© Flodden 1513 Club, Coldstream, Berwickshire, Scotland
www.Flodden1513club.com

by James Douglas Bell

ISBN 0 9546921 0 1

Printed by Kelso Graphics, Kelso, Roxburghshire, Scotland

Front Cover: The ring given to James IV by the Queen of France, to take three steps into England and break a lance for her.

CONTENTS

ACKNOWLEDGEMENTS

The 1513 Club without whose financial aid this book would still be on my PC

Gerald Tait, the scribe of that illustrious body

Susan, who helped so much in so many ways

Mary Poppins (Daff), who showed me around the City of London

David Ross of the Wallace Society

The Earl of Home

The Duke of Norfolk

Michelle Payne

The College of Arms (City of London)

The British Museum

Coldstream Museum

The late Vic Tokley

King James IV Committee

Everyone who has ever written a book on the battle or given me information

There are so many people who have helped and encouraged me on this venture that it would be impossible to thank them all individually.

Thank you all.

By buying this book about Flodden you are helping the 1513 Club maintain and preserve the traditions and the memory of what seems to many, the forgotten battle of our small nation. The Battle of Flodden.

My interest in Flodden started many years ago when as a young boy along with many others we used to cycle across to Flodden every year, following the Coldstreamer in the hope of being employed for an hour holding one of the many horses that had embarked on the annual pilgrimage from Coldstream to Flodden. Of course our reason for being there had nothing to do with some kind of historical remembrance, but to earn ten shillings or even a pound to spend at the shows on Saturday night. A few years later though, when I was 21 years old, I had the honour of leading the cavalcade to Flodden as Coldstreamer and the raw emotions that ran through my body that day are still vivid in my mind. The cheering crowds on Coldstream High Street, the Pipe Band playing Blue Bonnets over the Border, the 160 or so mounted followers who had come from all over the Borders and Northumberland to take part in the ride out. Then crossing the Tweed into England, not by one of the fords as had happened in 1513, but over the fine bridge that now spans the river. Riding over the beautiful Northumberland countryside, following the route taken by part of the Earl of Surrey's army many years ago. Passing by the Branx Brig, though at the time I did not know that, on into Branxton Village and stopping at the Flodden Memorial for the act of remembrance to the dead of both nations. It was then, it struck me, although there were quite a few spectators at the monument and hundreds on top of Branxton Hill, that the silence of the place was deafening. As I laid a wreath and the piper played The Flowers of the Forest, the tears for a long lost generation welled up inside me. From that moment on, Flodden became a big part of my life. I went on to become Chairman of Presenting Coldstream, the organisation that makes Coldstream Civic Week happen each year, though the Flodden Cavalcade and other mounted events are organised by the Coldstream Riders Association. As a fund raiser for Civic Week I presented a lecture assisted by slides on the battle, something I still do for history societies. The research for the lecture threw up more questions than answers about Flodden, and took me on a journey that has not finished yet.

I do hope that you enjoy *From Bourghmuir to Branxton Moor* and where there is a photo of empty farm land or a ruined pile of stones, use your imagination like I have, to take you back to those days of Flodden.

James Bell

INTRODUCTION

In 1919, at the end of the first Armistice Service on the 11th hour, of the 11th day, of the 11th month, at the Cenotaph in Whitehall, London, to remember the dead of the First World War, pipers of the Black Watch played a lament. Since then it has become a tradition at all War Memorials up and down Britain, and abroad, for the same tune to be played on Remembrance Sunday. That lament, the *Flowers of the Forest*, is most appropriate for the remembrance of the men who died in the terrible conflict known as "the war to end all wars". The *Flowers of the Forest* is the haunting lament for a generation of Scots who died on a lonely Northumberland hillside, in a battle that lasted about three hours, known as the Battle of Flodden.

Three miles across the River Tweed from the Scottish Border town of Coldstream, near the small Northumberland village of Branxton, stands a large granite monument in the shape of a cross. The inscription on the monument reads "The Battle Of Flodden, 9th September 1513, To The Brave of Both Nations". Other than a small information board, there is nothing to tell a visitor what happened in the surrounding fields. Here, nearly five hundred years ago, a King of Scotland and 10,000 of his subjects, including almost the whole ruling class of the nation and 4,000 Englishmen, mostly from the north of England, were killed in a battle that lasted three hours. Three hours of bloody hand to hand carnage, that left many a fatherless child, many a widow and a nation robbed of its nobility.

This is the story of Bloody Flodden.

The Flodden Memorial on Pipers' Hill at Branxton village.

WAR AND PEACE – PEACE AND WAR

James IV, the main character in the story of Flodden, was born on the 17th March,1473. He was crowned King of Scotland at Scone Abbey on the 26th June 1488 when his unpopular father, King James III, was killed after the Battle of Sauchieburn. Young James had taken up arms against his father along with Archibald Douglas the Earl of Angus, Lord Home and the Earl of Argyll. King James IV felt a terrible guilt for his part in his father's death, so much in fact, that he wore an iron chain on his body as a penance for the rest of his life. The chain was never found after the Battle of Flodden.

King James IV was one of the most popular monarchs that Scotland ever had. This is reflected in the number of men who joined him on his fatal venture into England in 1513.

The Flodden story starts on September 20th 1496, when a Scots Army led by King James IV invaded Northumberland, in support of Perkin Warbeck. Perkin Warbeck was a dreamer, who declared himself to James IV to be the son of Edward IV and therefore the legitimate heir to the English throne. Perkin Warbeck was also married to a relation of James, Lady Catherine Gordon, whom James had introduced to Warbeck. It seems that James was totally taken in by Warbeck, despite the efforts of the King and Queen of Spain to get James to give up Warbeck and ally with King Henry VII of England. Henry was already making plans to attack Scotland if James invaded England.

James IV used Warbeck's outrageous claim as an excuse to wage war on the English in Northumberland, also Warbeck had promised to return Berwick to Scotland when he became King of England. The first target of the Scots was Twizel Castle, pronounced *Twysel*. Twizel stood high above the River Till, a tributary of the Tweed, about four miles down stream from Coldstream, on the Cornhill to Berwick road. The ruins that stand there today are not the original, the tower that the Scots destroyed was just to the right of the present structure. Below the castle ruins stands Twizel Bridge, which itself had a decisive part to play in the Battle of Flodden. Looking northward from Twizel, towards the River Tweed and Scotland, is a place called Twizel Haugh, which also had an important part to play in the Flodden story.

The original Twizel Castle which the Scots destroyed belonged to the Heron family of Ford Castle.

After Twizel was taken and its defenders killed, Warbeck complained about the murder of his subjects, to which James replied, "*Considering you call England your land and realm, and the inhabitants there of, your people and subjects, not one English knight had shown himself or offered to assist you in this war, began for your cause and in your name*". Warbeck having been made to feel foolish by James in front of the Scottish nobles, fled back to Edinburgh, leaving James to continue the harassment and burning of Northumberland.

Duddo Tower.

From Twizel Castle the Scots moved south east towards Berwick, then attacked and destroyed Duddo Tower. From Duddo the Scots then turned south towards the Cheviots and marched along the eastern bank of the River Till, until they came to Etal Castle. Etal was in turn attacked and destroyed, though it was rebuilt a few years later only for the Scots to destroy the castle again in 1513.

Etal Castle.

The Scots next turned their attentions to the Howtel Tower, on the south side of Flodden Hill, to do this they would have crossed the River Till. From these ruins, with its seven foot thick walls, one can perceive what it must have been like in 1496. The only entrance into the twenty foot square tower is by an arched doorway, about five feet across. The floor has been built up through the centuries, or else the inhabitants and their cattle must have been of a miniature breed. I mention cattle, because these towers were designed that in times of trouble, the heavy door of the tower would be locked with the animals in the ground floor, while the defenders' living quarters were on the upper floors.

The first floor was usually made of stone, so that if the tower was set on fire, as happened often, the poor folk on the upper floor would have had some protection. Can you imagine the shock that William Burrell, who owned Howtel and his family got, when they saw the Royal Banner of Scotland at the head of a large body of men, intent on the destruction of their remote tower?

Howtel Tower.

After Howtel was attacked, the Scots turned and headed back towards the Border, going by way of Crookham, where on the 25th of September they destroyed Heaton Castle. The Scots then crossed back over the Tweed. King James and his subjects went home content, with their swords bloodied with English blood, their horses laden with English plunder.

This short campaign by King James IV was more of a large border raid, than a full scale invasion because he avoided any of the major English strongholds in the Border area, at Norham and Wark. It would also turn out to be almost a dress rehearsal for his Flodden campaign.

Perkin Warbeck, disappointed that none of the English Northern Lords joined him, sailed to Cornwall, in the South of England, to try to gain support there. By landing in Cornwall and raising a rebellion, Warbeck actually saved Scotland from King Henry sending an army north in retaliation for James's raid. Perkin Warbeck was eventually captured and executed for treason in 1499.

The next year 1497, the English raided in Berwickshire, the Scottish East March, the land of the Homes (pronounced Hume), a large and warlike family, who could turn out a force numbering into the thousands in less than three hours. The English found this out to their cost. The raiders were heavily defeated near Duns by Lord Home and his Borderers. The Homes can trace their descent from King Duncan, killed by MacBeth. Lord Home would lead the Scottish Vanguard at Flodden and in the twentieth century his descendant, Sir Alec Douglas Home, a great statesman, would as Prime Minister, become leader of Great Britain.

It is strange that on the English side of the Tweed, there are three major fortresses between the Border at Carham and where the Tweed empties into the North Sea, namely Wark, Norham and Berwick. But on the Scots side there are no major defensive towers or castles, until you are well into Berwickshire. There you will find an abundance of buildings and ruins, all belonging to, or having been owned by the Homes.

Encouraged by Home's success, King James IV issued orders for an army muster at Melrose. King James IV's artillery, including the famous Mons Meg which can still be seen in Edinburgh Castle, were hauled from the Castle and taken to Melrose. Large teams of oxen and horses, along with over 100 drivers were used to carry out this task. The Scots plan was to lay seige and destroy the important frontier stronghold of Norham Castle.

From Melrose, with its impressive Abbey, King James IV and his army followed the River Tweed downstream, passing through the Berwickshire village of Swinton. It was just outside Swinton that one of the carts used to carry Mons Meg's cannon balls sank in marsh where the Leet water runs. When the land was drained in 1870 the cart was found along with six of the cannon balls.

The church bell in Swinton which dates from 1499, was dedicated to the Blessed Virgin and is inscribed MARIA EST NOMEN MEUM, (MARY IS MY NAME) 1499. The bell, which is commonly known as the "Flodden Bell", was rung when some of the sad survivors of the battle passed through the village.

One of Mons Meg's cannon balls on the gate into a farm near Swinton.

Flodden Bell at Swinton Kirk.

The Scots army arrived at Ladykirk, opposite Norham Castle, in early August. The guns were positioned on the north bank of the River Tweed. There is a field named after Mons Meg on the local farm. With his artillery in position, King James IV and his army, forded the River Tweed, laid siege to Norham Castle before pillaging the surrounding countryside. During the time of Robert the Bruce, Norham had withstood many months of siege by the Scots. Prior to King James IV's siege Norham Castle's fortifications had recently been strengthened. Its garrison led by their Captain, Thomas Garth and the Bishop of Durham who had been in residence at the time, withstood all attempts of the Scots to take the fortress. One of Mons Meg's stone cannon balls, with a circumference of 51 inches, was found in the Tweed near to Norham Castle.

After ten days of siege, news reached the Scots that an English Northern Army, commanded by Thomas Howard, The Earl of Surrey, was on its way to relieve Norham Castle. The Scots withdrew back into Berwickshire.

Ladykirk takes its name from the impressive church called the Kirk of the Steill (salmon pool) that stands here. The romantic story is that King James IV after visiting one of his mistresses, Lady Heron of Ford Castle, almost drowned in a salmon pool at the West Ford of Norham. On being saved, he swore to build a church and dedicate it to the Virgin Mary. In reality, it was probably the Scots haste to reach their native soil, that led to King James IV almost drowning.

Ladykirk Church.

Sculpture of James IV on wall of Ladykirk Church. Illustration by Michelle Payne.

The English followed King James IV into Scotland, crossing the Border over the fords at Coldstream on the 16th of August, where they destroyed the village of Lennel. From Coldstream, the Earl of Surrey followed the Scots army to Ayton, destroying the Home tower of Edrington and the tower at Foul Dean [Foulden], before besieging Ayton Castle. After only two days Ayton fell to the Earl of Surrey. Apparently the Scots army was less than a mile away, but King James IV had seen his army grow smaller by the day, no doubt the Borderers having left taking as much plunder as they could carry home with them.

King James IV did not engage the much stronger English force with his army, but challenged Surrey to single combat – the victor would claim the town of Berwick. Surrey did not accept James's challenge, instead Surrey withdrew to Berwick on the 21st of August, without forcing the issue.

> *'I have not ridden in Scotland since*
> *James bask'd the cause of that mock prince,*
> *Warbeck, that Flemish counterfeit,*
> *Who on the gibbet paid the cheat.*
> *Then did I march with Surrey's power,*
> *What time we raised old Ayton tower.'*

> (Scott's Marmion)

From the Spanish Ambassador to the Scottish court, who had accompanied King James IV, we can get a glimpse of what King James IV was like. The Ambassador wrote *"James on this campaign is courageous even more than a king should be, I have seen him often undertake the most dangerous things in the last wars. I sometimes clung to his skirts to keep him back. He is not a good captain, because he begins to fight before he has given orders"*. It is also worth mentioning that around the time James became King, it is believed that the Spanish presented James with a sword and dagger, made from Toledo steel.

After his recent failure in England, King James IV's attitude to his larger neighbour changes rapidly. On the 30th September, a seven year truce was signed at Ayton, called the truce of Ayton, with both King James IV of Scotland and the English King Henry VII intent on keeping the peace. Among the twelve articles of the peace treaty, number seven states that *'the castle and town of Berwick.....stand free from attack from the King of Scots and his subjects; and that the King of England himself, or his subjects of the town of Berwick, abstain from war on the King of Scots or his lieges and vassals,'* also item eleven states that *'The Lordship of Lorne in Scotland and that of the Isle of Lundy in England are not comprehended in the present truce.'*

Even the murder of a number of Scots in July 1498, at Norham Castle, did not tempt James to break the truce. These Scots had swaggered into the castle and when challenged by the keeper of the castle as to their business there, there ensued a fight in which the Scots came off second best. The survivors, like a child having been bullied at school, ran back to Edinburgh and complained to King James. James did inform King Henry who said he would investigate the affair.

In 1496, King Henry VII had offered his daughter Margaret in marriage to King James IV, although James turned down this offer at the time. Negotiations for a marriage treaty were re-opened near the end of 1499 by Bishop Fox of Durham. King James IV was in fact engaged to Lord Drummond's daughter Margaret, who had bore him a daughter in 1497.

Margaret Drummond and her two sisters were poisoned in 1501 shortly before King James IV announced his intention to marry Margaret Tudor. Some historians say that James was in fact married to Margaret Drummond. She and her two sisters are buried side by side at Dunblane.

In October 1501, King James agreed to the marriage and the treaty. King James IV's marriage to Margaret Tudor was to bring about the first full peace treaty between Scotland and England for almost 170 years. This agreement was called The Treaty of Perpetual Peace.

'That between The Kings of Scotland and England, their heirs and successors, their kingdoms and subjects of every degree there be a good, real, sincere, true, sound and firm peace, friendship, league and confederation, to last to all time coming'.

The town of Berwick was also mentioned, as in the Truce of Aytoun, but the Isles of Lorne and Lundy were not.

The title alone would suggest that both parties wanted peace, but provisions were also made for regular diplomatic meetings on the frontier, to ensure no border incident escalated into full scale war and all fugitives were brought to justice. All future monarchs were to sign the treaty within six months of their coronation. The Pope in Rome also backed the treaty, when he declared that the first to break the treaty would be immediately excommunicated.

The marriage contract between King James IV of Scotland and Princess Margaret Tudor of England was signed on the 24th of January, 1502 at Richmond on Thames, by ambassadors of both parties. The next day the betrothal was announced at St. Paul's Cross in the City of London.

In the summer of 1503, the Princess Margaret, with four ladies in attendance left London for Edinburgh and her marriage to King James. She travelled in a carriage pulled by six grey horses, led by three men. There were about six hundred in the Princess's train. Her journey was carefully planned. She went by way of Grantham, Newark, Doncaster, Pontefract, Tadcaster, York, Newborough, Allerton, Durham, Hexham, Newcastle, Morpeth, Alnwick, Belford, Berwick, Lamberton Kirk, Fast Castle, Dunbar, Haddington, Dalkieth and finally to Edinburgh. Throughout her journey Princess Margaret was met and entertained by local gentry. On the 27th of July she left Morpeth in Northumberland. At Felton Bridge halfway between Morpeth and Alnwick, she was met by Harry Grey Esquire, Sheriff of Northumberland, with around one hundred of his men all dressed in his livery. At Berwick, Sir Thomas D'Arcy, the captain of the town ordered ordinance to be fired on the imminent arrival of the Princess. Near to Berwick the Princess dressed herself in more suitable clothing for entering a town as important as Berwick.

When the Princess's procession reached the bridge over the Tweed, it was met by Sir Thomas D'Arcy, with his men at arms. Waiting at the gate house was the Master Marshall with his company of men, each one carrying a halberd.

After she reached the Master Marshall, Margaret was given a cross to kiss by the Archbishop of York. On passing through the gate Margaret was then met by the Master Porter with a guard of honour, all in a row and well appointed with either halberds or a staff. On top of the gate were minstrels of the Captain playing music for the future Queen.

In the middle of the town Margaret was met by the Master Chamberlain and the Mayor, along with the burgesses and the inhabitants of the town. From here she was conveyed to the Castle where she was received by Lady D'Arcy. For two days Margaret stayed in Berwick, where she was well entertained by the Captain of Berwick.

In early August 1503, Princess Margaret, with her entourage of Lords, Ladies and Knights, led by The Archbishop of York and the Earl of Surrey crossed the Border where she was met by her future husband's representatives at St. Lambert's Kirk just north of Berwick. All the English Lords and Ladies in the procession were richly dressed in gold and precious stones. Even some of the horses' harnesses were made of gold.

King James IV met his 14 year old bride at Dalkieth. James kissed Margaret on their meeting and also made a special warm welcome to the Earl of Surrey.

The wedding of the Thistle and the Rose, as their union was called, was an extravagant affair in the Abbey Church of Holyrood. King James IV wore his robes of State, Queen Margaret was dressed in all her finery. The wedding was a merry celebration, with a fountain in Holyrood flowing with wine and there was great rejoicing in the City of Edinburgh. The English guests were treated to a great banquet with the best hospitality that was available in Scotland at that time. The Treaty of Perpetual Peace had now been completed.

James IV and his Queen Margaret on the old town cross of Galashiels.

In a letter to her father, King Henry, Margaret tells that *'our lord of Surrey is in great favour with the King here, that he cannot forbear the company of him no time of the day'*.

Margaret's dowry was £10,000, including the lands of Ettrick Forest and Cockburnspath, she also received an allowance of £2000 a year from King James IV. The lands of Ettrick Forest were handed over in front of local gentlemen and English representatives, including the Earl of Surrey, near the old town cross in Galashiels, by way of a ceremony where a sod and stone from the forest were handed over. In Cockburnspath, south of Dunbar, the Mercat Cross is a lasting memorial to the marriage. A thistle is carved on two sides, the other two have a rose.

The Perpetual Peace did not stop all incidents on the Border. In 1508, the Scottish Middle March Warden, Sir Robert Ker of Fernihurst, near Jedburgh, was killed at a March Wardens' meeting by John Heron, a nasty piece of work usually known as the 'Bastard Heron', and two accomplices. Because the wardens' meetings were held on a day of truce, this was a serious breach of the treaty. The two accomplices of Heron were caught and hanged, but Heron escaped and remained at liberty somewhere in the vast wilderness of the Cheviot Hills. The Bastard Heron's brother, Sir William Heron, master of Ford Castle was given up to the Scots as a hostage. William Heron was kept at the bleak Home stronghold of Fast Castle, high on the cliffs north of Eyemouth, until after the Scots were defeated at Flodden.

> *"Fast Castle if ye be ta'en*
> *Fair fa' you Johnny Robertson.*
> *Fast Castle firm and sure*
> *On rock will aye endure."*
> *(Old poem on the Scots taking control of the castle by use of disguise)*

King Henry VII's biggest concern with his son in law was the navy King James IV was building. James loved military toys like ships and cannon. James's first big ship "The Margaret" was launched in 1506 and in the two years before the Battle of Flodden, James was spending a vast amount of money, around £9000 a year on new ships. Much of the material and the craftsmen that were used to build the Scottish fleet were provided by Louis XII of France.

King Henry VII died in 1509 and was succeeded by his son Henry VIII, who signed the Treaty of Perpetual Peace within the stipulated six month period of his coronation.

In May of that year, relations between Scotland and England must still have been reasonable, for King James in a royal letter under the Privy Seal, gave permission to the Prioress and nuns of Coldstream convent, to *"intercommoun with Inglesmen in bying or selling of vittalis, sheip and other legal gudis,"*. Permission was also granted to receive up to twelve persons from England, allowing them to come and go as they please.

Henry VIII though, was an entirely different man from his father, it was not long before King James IV and he had disagreements. Henry's sister, the Scots Queen Margaret had been left jewels in her father's estate. She sent several letters to King Henry VIII asking for her inheritance to be sent to Scotland. Henry eventually sent an ambassador with a message to James; "..*the legacy will be sent if the King of Scots makes a solemn promise to keep the peace treaty...*" he also threatened that if the King of Scots refused, King Henry VIII would not only keep the jewellery, but would take the best towns he had in Scotland.

Old scores soon came to the fore, including the failure of the English government to detain the Bastard Heron.

In 1511, King James IV's largest warship, "The Great Michael" was launched. She had a crew of 300, carried 27 big guns with 120 'gunners'. "The Great Michael" was one of the finest ships of her time and an alarming threat to the English Navy. "The Great Michael" had a displacement of 1000 tons compared to the 600 tons of King Henry's flag ship the "Mary Rose".

On the 2nd of August, 1511, an incident took place that was going to gall King James IV in two years time. Two Scots vessels, "The Lion" and "The Jenny Pirwin", commanded by one of King James IV's favourite captains Sir Andrew Barton, were attacked by an English force led by Edward and Thomas Howard, the Earl of Surrey's sons. In a desperate fight, Barton was killed and his ships taken as a prize.

King James IV sent a letter complaining to King Henry VIII demanding compensation. King Henry VIII replied that "*.. Barton was a pirate and that Kings ought not to concern themselves with the fate of pirates and thieves.*" Henry came to this conclusion about Barton from letters he received from John, King of Denmark. The Danish King complained to Henry that Barton had been sent to Denmark by King James to serve with the Danish navy. Barton had left without leave, taking with him a ship which James had gifted to King John.

King Henry's letter infuriated King James IV even more. James wrote to Pope Jullius II in Rome, citing the Barton and Heron incidents as clear evidence of the King of England's aggression towards Scotland, demanding King Henry VIII's excommunication, and the Scots King to be absolved from his oath and free to retaliate. Pope Julius did not reply!

At Embleton Bay, in Northumberland, depending on exceptional tides, there appears a flat rock of about five yards square. Andrew Barton's name, among others, is carved on this rock.

Edward Howard was appointed Lord Admiral of England in 1512, and in April 1513 he rashly attacked the French Admiral Pregent off Brest in Brittany. Edward Howard boarded the Admiral's ship, but his own ship was carried away by the tide, leaving him stranded. Howard threw his badge of office, a golden whistle into the sea, before jumping himself. His older brother Thomas was made Lord Admiral on Edward's death.

A major dispute that had been simmering for some time, erupted in Europe, when Pope Jullius and King Ferdinand of Spain, formed a Holy League against Louis XII of France. In November 1511, King Henry VIII joined the Holy League against France, and in January 1512 Emperor Maximillian of Austria joined the allies. King James IV saw this dispute as a chance for him to show the rest of Europe what a great statesman he was, he attempted to act as peace broker between France and the Pope. Unfortunately he failed, because the members of the Holy League were determined to fight with France.

King James IV now found himself in a difficult position. Scotland's old ally, France, was being threatened by his brother-in-law.

In 1512, King Henry VIII revived the English claim of over-lordship of Scotland. This was last used by King Edward IV in 1482, and this pushed King James IV to renew the Auld Alliance with France.

King Louis sent his ambassador, Charles de La Mothe, to negotiate the terms of the treaty with James IV. On his way to Scotland, La Mothe engaged a number of English merchant ships, he sent three to the bottom of the sea, captured several others and brought them to the port of Leith in Edinburgh.

During the year 1513 all the countries involved in the Holy League dispute prepared for war.

In Scotland, King James IV's master gunner, Robert Borthwick, was busy in the foundry of Edinburgh Castle making new cannon and ammunition, no doubt the Borderers were seizing the chance to make mischief on their neighbours.

During a debate in the Scottish Council, William Elphinstone, Bishop of Aberdeen, and old Archibald Douglas, Earl of Angus, two of the most respected gentlemen in Scotland, spoke out against the war preparations. However, after a heated debate the Council agreed to France's plea for help. Queen Margaret also tried to dissuade her husband from going to war; "I *beseech you to spare me from the unnatural spectacle of seeing my husband arrayed in mortal combat against my brother."*

King Henry had sent an ambassador to the Scottish Court in March of 1513. His name was Nicholas West and his job was to inform Henry of any developments in Scotland. West was really a spy. On April 1st he wrote to Henry after a meeting with James at Stirling, reporting that James had told him that; *"he (James) would never make you war without he warn you before by his Herald, so that you shall have time enough, though you were in France, to come and defend your own."* In the same letter West states that James had shown him a letter signed by the King of France, where *"James was to be granted the levies from one tenth of the King of France's realm, and also a number of men of arms and footmen, and shipping convenient for the number of men that he will have with him."*

West in a another letter to Henry in April, states that at the harbour of Newhaven, James's ship "The Michael" *is being prepared for sea.*

King Louis of France gave King James money and thousands of eighteen foot pikes. He also sent 50 captains to train the Scots in the use of these weapons. These long pikes were a favourite weapon being used by European armies.

In May the French army advanced on Milan, while Henry VIII made ready to invade France. The French Queen sent King James IV a letter. She asked for his protection against English attack, to march forth, even if it were only three feet on English soil, and break a lance for her sake. She sent James a further 14,000 gold crowns, also as a personal gesture to James, she sent a gold and turquoise ring from her hand which King James IV wore until his death.

In June 1513, the English army sailed for Calais. King Henry VIII knew the threat from Scotland would be real, so he instructed the now seventy year old Earl of Surrey, the Earl Marshal of England and lieutenant-general to the north, to watch the northern border. His orders were to meet any aggression with aggression. Surrey was not happy with this order as he felt he should have been beside his King fighting in France.

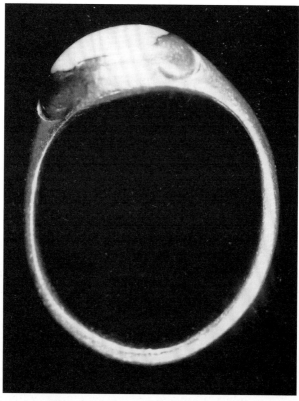

Ring sent to James IV by French Queen.

As part of the alliance with France, the Scottish fleet was to sail to France to help the French navy against the English. In July, the Scottish fleet set sail, commanded by the Earl of Arran. Arran sailed near to the Irish coast, attacking the Ulster fortress of Carrickfergus, which was in the hands of the English. James had sent some of his most experienced gunners with the fleet to France. Andrew Barton's brother John sailed with the fleet to France, no doubt looking for revenge for his brother's death, but he fell ill and had to be put ashore near Kirkcudbright in south west Scotland, where he died of his illness.

In times of invasion, a fiery cross would be sent round the country to rally the people to King's standard, but it is not documented if this method was used in 1513. King James IV sent heralds to the north, south, east and west of his kingdom to summon all men aged between 16 and 60. They were to assemble fully armed with provisions, between the 13th and the 20th of August, at the Boroughmuir in Edinburgh.The men from the Borders to meet the army at Ellem Kirk, just north of Duns in Berwickshire.

The Earl of Surrey was also busy preparing for his journey north. Surrey was gathering his private army of about 500 men drawn from his estates. All Surrey's men were paid retainers, and converting the sums to today's equivalent, it seems that they were very well paid.

These men were led by five captains who were paid 4 shillings a day, the petty captains were paid 2 shillings a day. The Solitary Spear, Earl Surrey's Standard Bearer, earned 1 shilling and 6 pennies a day. The rest of the Earl of Surrey's personal force were paid 8 pennies a day. The Earl of Surrey's head-quarter staff was made up of 39 men. The Earl's youngest son Edmund Howard was 'Marshall of the Host' and the 'Master of Ordinance' was Sir Nicholas Appleyard. The artillery train had about 400 drivers and 24 guns. The rest of the Earl Surrey's force included a Herald, six trumpeters, clerks, guards, servants and a joiner. The joiner presumably was there to make repairs to the gun carriages and the like.

The Earl of Surrey left London on the 21st of July and headed north to Pontefract Castle, which he made his headquarters. Surrey because of his age, travelled in a carriage.

On the 26th of July, King James IV sent the Lyon King at Arms, to France firstly to inform the French Queen, that the Scottish fleet had set sail for Brest. On receiving this information, Queen Anne's three ships plus eight others were to be prepared immediately and to set sail to join the Scots fleet off Normandy. It was observed that they must be prompt *as the season passes*.

The Lord Lyon then went to Therouanne in France, where King Henry VIII's army were besieging the town. On the 11th of August the Herald delivered the King of Scotland's message to King Henry. The following details of that meeting are taken from the State Papers of Henry VIII.

The 11 day of August, 1513, the King being in his rich tent, the herald of the King of Scots was brought to him and gave his message (recited) that, having now besieged Turwyn two months without being fought with and having, by his invasion, caused the King of France to recall his army from Milan, Henry should be content and return home without making further war. *"The King, standing still with sober countenance, having his hand on his sword, said 'Have ye now your tale at an end?' The herald of arms said 'Nay'. 'Say forth then,' said the King. 'Sir, he summoneth your grace to be at home in your realm in the defence of his ally.'* Then the King answered and said *'Ye have well done your message; nevertheless it becometh ill a Scot to summon a King of England. And tell your master that I mistrust not so the realm of England but he shall have enough to do whensoever he beginneth; and also I trusted no him not so well but that I provided for him right well, and that shall he well know, and he summoned me, now being here for my right and inheritance! It would much better agreed with his honour to have summoned me being at home; for he knew well before my coming hither that hither I would come. And now he send me summons! Tell him there shall never a Scot cause me to return my face. And where he layeth the French King to be his ally it would much better agreed and become him, being married to the King of England's sister, to recount the King of England his ally. And now, for a conclusion, recommend me to your master and tell him if he be so hardy to invade my realm or cause to enter one foot of my ground I shall make him as weary of his part as ever was man that began any such business. And one thing I ensure him by the faith that I have to the Crown of England and by the word of a King, there shall never King nor Prince make peace with me that ever his part shall be in it. Moreover, fellow, I care for nothing but for misentreating of my sister, that would God she were in England on a condition she cost the Scots King not a penny.'* The Herald answered and said *' If your grace would give her your whole realm she would foresake it to be entreated as she is,'* The King said *'I know the contrary and know what all this matter meaneth; the King your master has been anointed with the crowns of the sun, but I trust er it be long the French King shall have enough to do to keep his crowns for himself."*

From this document it would appear that the French had sent an army to Milan against the Pope, and on the English invading France, the French army withdrew from its campaign. Also King Henry was accusing the Scots of mistreating his sister Queen Margaret. This seems to be a common thought amongst the English and is mentioned in a poem called *Flodden Field*. Henry also warns the Scots against invading England, or else face the consequences.

Perhaps it was King Henry who coined the phrase that you can pick your friends, but you cannot pick your relations!

Meanwhile the Earl Surrey had arrived at Pontefract Castle and was recruiting his army from all parts of the North.

On the Border things were starting to hot up! In early August, English Borderers made a large raid into Berwickshire, crossing the fords at Coldstream causing much damage and taking considerable plunder. The Scots response was swift and hard. Lord Home, who by this time had the title of Lord High

Chamberlain of Scotland and Warden of the Border Marches, retaliated by leading a force of no less than 3000 mounted Borderers across the Tweed into Northumberland. They raided well down beyond Wooler, which is 17 miles across the border. They burned four villages, collected a large herd of horses and cattle, before making back for Scotland, laden with plunder. The Borderers had so much booty that their ride home was slow and cumbersome.

A Northumberland force raised by Sir William Boulmer, of about 200 archers and 800 horsemen, circled ahead of the Scots. They laid an ambush at the foot of Humbleton Hill between Wooler and Milfield, near to the spot where the Northumberland Percy and the Scots Douglas had clashed many years before, this battle had much the same outcome.

View from Humbleton hill towards the Borders.

As Home's Borderers came over the track from Wooler Common, down Humbleton Hill, the English were hidden in the natural thick broom of Milfield plain. When the English arrows fell on the Scots, confusion set in. Again and again the archers sent their deadly arrows into the Scots, then the English cavalry charged. The Scots fled leaving behind their booty.

The English claimed that up to 500 of Home's Borderers were killed and over 400 taken prisoner. Including Lord Home's brother George, they also captured the Home standard. The capturing of an enemy's standard seems to be more significant that the amount of men who are lost. This defeat happened only weeks before the battle of Flodden, and became known as "the III Raid" or "the III Rode".

FROM BOROUGHMUIR TO BRANXTON MOOR

King James' subjects flocked to his summons, some say as many as 100,000 gathered on the Boroughmuir, where Morningside stands today. The population of Scotland at the time was only about 500,000, so this number of 100,000 seems to be grossly exaggerated.

The night before the Scots army was to leave Edinburgh, a mysterious voice could be heard in the cannon gate of the town, proclaiming a list of names of those who would not return from the King's venture. Previous to this, James had been confronted by an apparition while he was at prayer in Linlithgow Palace. These two occurrences were put down to the Queen's attempts to stop the war with England before it had started.

The Bore Stone on which the Royal Standard was raised.

The Boroughmuir was a spacious field, and walking amongst this mass of men, one would have heard so many different Scots dialects. It was here on the Boroughmuir, that most of the 17,000 inhabitants of Edinburgh came to view the largest and finest Scots army ever assembled and to see the Royal Standard raised by Sir Andrew Foreman, the King's Standard Bearer. This grand army with King James IV's pride, Robert Borthwick's guns, including seven identical brass cannon called the seven sisters, left Edinburgh for Ellem Kirk on the 17th of August.

King James IV left on the 19th, and the whole army including the Border men met at Ellem Kirk, 14 miles from the Border on the evening of the 20th August.

Ellem Ford.

Many Border men, including the 80 men from the Royal Burgh of Selkirk, assembled at the Home castle of Bunkle, about five miles east of Ellem Kirk, before making their way to meet the King.

An old local poem attributed to Thomas the Rymer made a couple of hundred years before, mentions Bunkle Castle and a prophecy which has come true.

> *"Bunkle, Billie, and Blanerne,*
> *Three castles strang as airn,*
> *Built when Davy was a bairn,*
> *They'll a' gang doon*
> *Wi' Scotlands croon,*
> *And ilka ane sall be a cairn".*

All that remains of Bunkle Castle.

The three castles were destroyed by the Earl of Hertford in 1545.

Bunkle Castle judging from what can be seen of it, must have been a strong fortress, with commanding views to the south.

The Scottish army spent the night in the town of Duns. It is said that James held his last Parliament on Scottish soil here.

River Tweed at Coldstream, with Branxton Hill on the Skyline.

On the 22nd of August, this great host, the vanguard led by Lord Home, crossed the fords of the River Tweed at Coldstream and Lennel, of which there were seven or eight. The fords over the Tweed at Coldstream, were the first fordable places on the river, with relatively flat ground on either side. Even so it was still a dangerous crossing point. The river has changed so much since the days that the ford was used, that it is only fordable when the river is very low, even then it is not recommended.

On their first night on English soil, the Scots camped at Twizel Haugh, a flat piece of ground behind Twizel Castle, which James had visited in 1496. Just below Twizel, the Tweed is at its deepest on its winding way to the sea. It was on the haugh of Twizel that James, under pressure from his noblemen, proclaimed that any man killed in this war would not have to pay any feudal death duty. This was normally done after a battle, but on this occasion it was done before. Perhaps King James's noblemen had an inkling of the disaster that would befall them.

On crossing the Border with his army James had broken the Treaty of Perpetual Peace and was now effectively excommunicated.

The next morning, the Scots Army was split in two, with one half and the guns moving on Norham Castle, while the other moving on the much weaker Wark Castle.

In its time Wark had been the staging post for many an English invasion of Scotland, and many a bloody fight took place around its walls. Legend has it

Twizel Haugh.

that one of England's greatest orders of chivalry, the Order of the Garter was started here. King Edward 111, his Queen and their court were at Wark in 1348. One night while dancing in the great hall of the castle, the Countess of Salisbury one of the Queen's ladies in waiting, dropped her garter. Amongst the mirth of the incident, the King picked up the embarrassed Countess's garter, held it aloft, saying *"Honi soit qui mal y pense"* (evil be to him who thinks evil), thus silencing those laughing at the Countess's expense. Historians will say this is a lot of rubbish, as the Order of the Garter was inaugurated at Windsor Castle, but who is to say that King Edward did not get his idea from the incident at Wark.

The Keep of Wark Castle from the Scots side of the Tweed.

In the Tweed below Wark Castle is an Island known as Treaty Island. This is where the Treaty of Birgham was signed, confirming Margaret the Maid of Norway as the successor to the Scottish throne.Unfortunatly Margaret died at Orkney before she could take her throne, and this left the way open for Edward Longshanks of England to pursue his ambitions in Scotland.

Close by to Wark is the village of Carham, here there took place two battles. One was between the Vikings and Saxons, where the outnumbered Vikings slaughtered the badly armed Saxons, the second between was between Scots, who heavily defeated their English opponents. That battle decided the border between England and Scotland that we know today.

Some days before the Scots invaded England in 1513, two banners were removed from Wark to the stronger fortress of Berwick for safe keeping. These banners were the War Banners of The Knights Of The Temple. The first is called "VEXILLUM BELLI" – war banner of the Knights of the Temple, the second is called "BEACEANT" – war cry of the Knights of the Temple. The banners are about thirty inches long by sixteen inches wide, with a Germanic cross on the top part, the length falling to two tails, and are kept in Berwick to this day.

By 1513, Wark's defences had been allowed to deteriorate and it fell easily to the Scots.

Norham Castle in 1318 had withstood almost two years of siege by King Robert Bruce, but now its old thick walls had to withstand the cannonade that the Borthwicks guns threw at it from close range.

Legend has it that an English traitor slipped out of the castle and gave the Scots information of the weakest parts of the defences.

Eventually the Scots broke through the outer walls, but the inner keep held out until the 29th of August, when out of ammunition, the English commander, John Ainslow was forced to surrender.

The English informer, legend has it, was rewarded by King James IV with a rope around his neck. There is a field close by known as "hangman's field."

Norham Castle.

After Norham Castle fell, up to 25,000 Scots left the army and went home, many with their saddlebags full of booty. Thomas Ruthall the Bishop of Durham, wrote to Wolsey before the Battle of Flodden with the heading *"This letter is sorrowful and the other conformable"* '*that the King of Scots had sieged, 'saulted and in a great stormy night scaled and won the castle of Norham; which news touched me so near with inward sorrow that I had lever to have been out of the world than in it, especially as I had been assured of its security by Will Pawne and others. He shall never forget it or recover from grief. Will trust, however, within five years, to set 10,000 marks upon it, though he take penance and live a more moderate life. I never felt the hand of God so sore touching me as in this, whereof I most humbly thank him, and, after the inward search of conscience to know the cause of this provocation of Gods displeasure against me, I shall reform it, if it lie in my power and regard Him more than the world hereafter"*.

At the end of the letter, The Bishop added in his own hand *"this letter was written before the Battle, which I reserved in hope of better tidings, which God hath now sent,"*

In a further letter to Wolsey, Ruthall describes the damage to the castle; *"..need not rehearse his sorrow that his, (Henry VIII) of Norham has been, by the cruel tyranny of The King of Scots, razed to the ground. Will study how to renew it. The dungeon stands, and part of the wall..."*

Walking amongst the Norham Castle ruins, in the solitude of a winters' afternoon, you can almost hear the cannon fire and the cries of invaders as they scramble over the castle walls.

Etal Castle.

From Norham, the Scots moved along the east bank of the River Till, following the same well worn route as they had when they invaded England with Perkin Warbeck in 1496, to the now rebuilt Etal Castle, which again fell easily to the mighty Scots army.

Once Etal fell, the Scots then turned their attention on Ford Castle. Ford Castle was defended by Lady Heron, whose husband was still a hostage of Scotland in Fast Castle. Some time before the Scots had arrived, Lady Heron had asked Earl Surrey for help. Earl Surrey had offered to release important prisoners, including Lord Home's brother captured at Humbleton, if the Castle was spared. The offer was rejected and the castle stormed. Lady Heron was now King James's prisoner. King James IV made Ford Castle his base where he kept, according to Lady Heron, about 10,000 men at arms, while the majority of his army pillaged the surrounding countryside. Legend has it that James and Lady Heron were on intimate terms, and it was her who made James remove the iron chain he wore at all times, as she found it very uncomfortable whilst making love. It is also said Lady Heron was sending secret information about the Scots to the Earl of Surrey.

Ford Castle, the Lefthand Tower was where James IV stayed.

King James's infatuation with Lady Heron is one of the reasons that was put forward for James not advancing further south into northern England. If you remember that James had already fought a campaign over this land many years before, and Ford being quite close to the Border and the Scots supply line, it quite reasonable to come to the conclusion that James never intended to go beyond Ford.

Flodden Hill now covered in woodland.

While at Ford, King James IV and his advisors knew the English would soon be closing in for battle, so they moved the army and guns a short distance across the River Till by way of an old bridge, to the large hill known as Flodden Hill. The army encamped on the top of the hill, while the guns were placed in 3 large pits dug in the hillside, facing towards Ford Castle. Although the hill is now woodland, the gun emplacements can still be seen in the side of Flodden Hill.

With their guns dug in on Flodden hill, the Scots now had a commanding view over the surrounding countryside. The Scots also ravished and plundered the surrounding countryside. Places today which are just farms were small villages and hamlets in the 16th century. Places like Howtel, Moneylaws and Downham are close by the battlefield, but these Border hamlets in time of war were deserted and left to the invaders.

The weather since the Scots had invaded England had not been good, and it had rained almost every single day. More and more men left the army until it was reduced to around 30,000. Still a powerful force, as those that were left were the best fighting men in all of Scotland.

Meanwhile, news of the Scots invasion reached the Earl of Surrey. Surrey sent messages to all the Northern Lords and Gentry to muster at Newcastle on the 1st of September.

The next day Surrey himself left Pontefract for Newcastle, calling at York, where the Lord Mayor was ordered to muster all the city's men at arms and proceed to Newcastle. A large amount of money was collected from the Abbot of St Mary's, presumably to buy provisions or payment for his troops. On the 29th, August Surrey reached Durham, to be told the news that Norham Castle had fallen to the Scottish army.

One of the Scots gun emplacements on Flodden Hill.

Surrey arrived at Newcastle on the 30th of August, where he was met by Lord Dacre, Warden of the English West March (Cumberland and Westmoreland), Sir William Boulmer who had defeated Lord Home at Humbleton, and Sir Marmaduke Constable. Constable had been Henry VII's commissioner in Scotland, and had accompanied Queen Margaret to her wedding. The weather had turned nasty, with heavy rain and strong winds. The Lord Admiral, Surrey's son, was on his way to join his father with ships from the fleet, but had not arrived due to the bad weather and this was of some concern to the Earl, having already lost his son Edward in April of that year.

Over the next couple of days the English army was growing larger by the hour. Sir Edward Stanley brought 8,500 men from Lancashire, there were also men from Cheshire, Yorkshire and Humberside. All these, together with the men from Durham, Northumberland and Cumbria, the English army packed into Newcastle, totalled over 24,000.

By the 2nd of September, the English had advanced to a place called Bolton in Glendale, just north of Alnwick. The land at Bolton is flat, and one can imagine line upon line of tents that made up the English camp. On the 3rd of September, Thomas Howard The Admiral arrived, and brought with him around 2,000 marines from the fleet and a number of mercenary gunners from Danzig in Germany.

On the 4th, Surrey and his generals decided to send the Rouge-Croix Herald (red cross) to King James, inviting him to do Battle.

Heralds were used as diplomats, army staff officers and messengers. The use of Heralds dates back to the First Crusade. Heralds became experts in identifying army commanders and men of importance, by recognising the Coats of Arms and devices painted on shields, banners and surcoats, as it was impossible to recognise someone with a war helmet on. Through time the Heralds also became experts in organising great state occasions, and even today the Heralds come under the direction of the Duke of Norfolk (Earl of Surrey), the hereditary Earl Marshall of England. They are responsible for organising the great state occasions in London, like the state opening of Parliament and state funerals. There are different ranks of heralds, The Kings of Herald or Kings of Arms, the next rank is Heralds, while the junior rank is called Pursuivant. These ranks still exist today for the thirteen Officers at Arms, based in the College of Arms in the City of London, not far from St Paul's Cathedral. The Rouge-Croix Herald was a junior rank.

The main concern of the English commanders was to bring the Scots to battle as soon as possible, not let them retreat over the Border as had happened the last time the Earl of Surrey's northern army had tried to fight King James IV, in 1497. Surrey was also worried about the lack of provisions for his army, the Scots having plundered North Northumberland bare.

If two countries went to war in our time, there would be a flurry of diplomatic peace envoys to try and avoid any blood shed, but in the 16th century it was entirely the opposite. Both parties arranged a time and a place for the fight, like a pair of duellists, except on a larger scale.

The Rouge-Croix Herald, Thomas Hawley, was to carry two letters to King James IV. The first letter was from the Earl of Surrey, chastising King James IV for invading his brother-in-law's realm, for burning, spoiling, destroying and cruelly murdering the King's subjects, and Surrey challenged James to do battle on the vast flat ground of Milfield Plain, on the 9th September.

The second letter was from Thomas Howard, The Admiral. The Admiral first taunted King James IV that his great navy had crept away to France, rather than fight his English ships, and then the Admiral reminded King James IV that it was he who had defeated Sir Andrew Barton, and was responsible for Barton's death. That evening the Herald rode out for Ford Castle.

On the morning of the 5th August on the flat ground of Bolton, the English Army was marshalled into battle order of two main divisions, the vanguard and the rearguard. Each division was to have two wings. The vanguard was to be commanded by Thomas Howard, the Admiral, and the rearguard by the Earl Surrey himself. King Henry's Royal Standard of a Red Dragon and the Sacred Banner of St Cuthbert, brought from Durham by Bishop Ruthall, were raised at Bolton.

It is worth mentioning that at the time of Flodden, England had three armies in the field. There was the army with King Henry in France, Surrey's army at Flodden and Henry's Queen Katherine was at the head of an army of similar size to that of Surrey's. It is fair to assume that the Queen's army would have went to face the Scots had Surrey been defeated. Queen Katherine was near Birmingham when word reached her of Surrey's victory.

Herald Thomas Hawley reached Ford Castle, only to find it partially destroyed, King James was by now with the Scots army on Flodden Hill. King James IV was not amused by the letters Surrey and the Admiral had sent, but secure in his position he agreed to fight on the 9th of September. As not to reveal the Scots strength, the English Herald was kept at the Scottish camp and a Scottish Herald, Lord Islay, was sent to Earl Surrey with King James IV's reply.

Lord Islay, accompanied by a Borderer acting as a guide, arrived at Bolton late on the evening of the 5th, and were kept overnight at the English camp.

Surrey and his generals met Lord Islay in the morning. The Earl of Surrey, was over the moon that King James IV had agreed to fight, but he was also angered that James had kept his Herald prisoner. Surrey in turn detained Lord Islay at his camp, sending the Scots guide back to King James IV with a message, demanding Thomas Hawley be released immediately. The English Herald was released as was Lord Islay when Hawley returned to the English army at Bolton.

Thomas Hawley reported that the Scots army was at least 40,000 strong, also that the Scots were in a strong position on Flodden Hill. With information from local men, it was clear to Surrey that the Scots position was immense.

Surrey immediately ordered his troops to march to Wooler. On reaching Wooler the English camped the night of the 6th on Wooler Haugh. Surrey stayed in a house that still stands beside the main road to Newcastle. It is a ramshackle of a building, having had bits added here and there over the years, but to the rear can be seen some of the original stones. It is still known today as Surrey House.

Ruins of Surrey House, Wooler Haugh.

Late that evening a band of horsemen entered the camp, demanding to see Surrey. This was the outlaw John Heron, the Bastard of Ford. Heron asking to join Surrey's army, and that he be pardoned for his crimes. Heron was allowed to stay, but was not pardoned at this time.

Surrey and his generals decided to send King James IV another message. So, at around 5 o'clock in the afternoon of the 7th September, Thomas Hawley was sent back to Flodden Hill with Surrey's message once more inviting King James IV to fight on Milfield Plain by noon on the 9th, but Surrey also bitterly complained that the Scots had taken a position more like a fortress.

King James IV this time refused to see the English Herald, but gave his reply, *"that he would fight by noon on the 9th, but he would take and keep his ground and field at his pleasure, and not at the assigning of an Auld and Crookit Earl"*.

Milfield Plain from Doddington Hill, Flodden Hill is on the extreme right.

Surrey must have had second thoughts about fighting James on Milfield plain or he knew James would not come down off Flodden Hill, because on the morning of the 8th, the English left Wooler and headed north by way of Doddington, a large hill dominating Wooler in the valley below, with the River Till between them and the Scots. For a short time the two armies would have been able to see their adversaries. By late afternoon the English had disappeared from the Scots view behind the hills beyond Ford, they made their camp at Barmoor Wood, near Lowick.

The tower at Barmoor was owned and inhabited by George Muschamps and could accommodate thirty men. No doubt these men were removed of their beds in favour of Surrey and his captains.

There is in existence an old drawing of the Earl of Surrey at camp on the morning of the battle, the name of the camp is given as Bermer wood, by Twyselford.

The watching Scots were puzzled by the direction Surrey had taken; was he heading for Berwick, or even towards the undefended Border? James made his first mistake at this time by not sending any mounted scouts to watch the English armies' movements. Auld Archibold Douglas urged the King to withdraw back to Scotland, but King James dismissed Douglas's pleadings, saying *"Angus, if you are afraid you may go home"*. A reproach which drove old Angus to tears, telling his King *"my age renders my body of no service, and my council is despised, but I leave two sons and the vassals of Douglas in the field, may the result be glorious, and Angus's foreboding unfounded,"*

The Earl of Surrey at prayer on the morning of the Battle.

Barmoor Castle.

That evening a group of riders appeared on a hill near Etal, known today as Watch Law. The Admiral and some of his officers, accompanied by some local gentlemen, John Heron, The Bastard among them, were studying the Scots position. It was clear a frontal assault would be suicidal, but Heron, who knew the countryside like the back of his hand, advised his countrymen that they could get between Flodden Hill and the Border, cut off the Scots line of retreat and therefore forcing them to fight. It was also observed that if they could climb the lesser Branxton Hill, the English would have a more level ground to fight on.

Flodden Hill from Watchlaw.

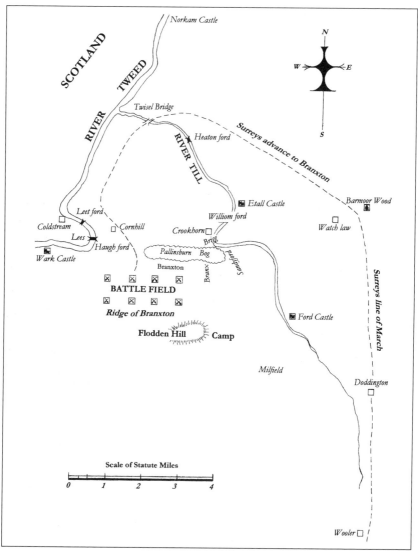

Illustration by Michelle Payne.

The next part of the Flodden story is where most historians disagree. It is known that the English vanguard and the artillery crossed Twizel Bridge, and went by way of the village of Donaldson's Lodge and Cornhill before turning south towards Branxton. A march of some 12 miles. However historians give us three options for the rearguard's advance to Branxton.

The first option is that the rearguard would separate from the vanguard and go by way of Watch Law and cross the Till at Sandyford near the village of Crookham, with the two parts of the army joining up at the Crookham Moor Gathering Stone, a large stone which stands close to the main road near to the farm of Crookham West Field. This stone is known locally as the King's Stone, supposedly as the place where King James was either killed or buried. But this stone was standing here many centuries before Flodden.

Crookham Moor gathering stone.

The second option that we are asked to contemplate is that the rearguard followed the vanguard, but crossed the Till, a mile up stream from Twizel at Mill Ford, below where Heaton Castle stands.

The third option is that the rearguard followed the vanguard across Twizel Bridge, and then the two divisions split, and the rearguard following the River Till, still in view of the vanguard, and crossing the Pallins Burn near to where it empties into the Till at Sandyford.

The first option leads us to ask why Surrey, such a seasoned military man, would risk his entire force, by sending one half of his army miles away from the other half, leaving them to the mercy of the Scots, because Surrey did not know that James did not have scouts watching his every move. The River Till also comes into the equation. It has been documented that it had rained nearly every day since the Scots invaded, and the Till would have been running high. The river is a dangerous river at the best of times, and there is an old poem which describes it quite well.

> *'Tweed said to Till*
> *'What gars ye rin sae still':*
> *Till said to Tweed*
> *'Though ye rin wi speed,*
> *An' I rin slaw,*
> *For ilka man ye droon,*
> *I droon twa'*

So although this theory of Surrey sending the vanguard by Twizel and the rearguard by Etal to Crookham is quoted in many books, I doubt if this did happen.

In the second option, the flooded River Till again casts doubt that the Mill Ford would have been used by troops marching on foot, although horsemen might have been able to cross, but as most of the English army marched on foot from Barmoor Wood to Branxton, this would rule out Mill Ford.

This leaves option three as the most probable route that the English rearguard used.

> *'And never flee while life did last*
> *But rather die by dint of sword*
> *Thus over plains and hills they passed*
> *Until they come to Sandyford'*

The above verse is from an old poem written about 30 years after the battle and describes the English rearguard's advance to Crookham.

Twizel Bridge.

Thomas Howard the Admiral, wrote to King Henry giving his account of the Battle of Flodden. This document is called the Articles of Batyle. In this letter the Admiral states that his father and the rearguard followed the vanguard over Twizel Bridge.

That evening the Admiral told his father the Earl of Surrey of the plan. It was decided that once the vanguard and artillery had crossed Twizel Bridge, they would continue west until they reached the village of Donaldson's Lodge, or more likely Cornhill, then turn south towards Branxton and the Scots army camped of Flodden Hill. Surrey and the rearguard would also cross Twizel Bridge, then advance to Branxton through where Tillmouth Park Hotel is today, and follow the River Till past Castle Heaton to Crookham, thus getting the whole English army totally behind the Scots. That night as the rain again fell heavily, both armies would have spent an uncomfortable night. The English army were almost out of provisions, especially ale, and were forced to drink muddy water, with what food they had.

THE BATTLE OF FLODDEN

At about 5.00am on the day of the battle, 14,000 men and 24 cannon of the vanguard set off north-westwards for Twizel Bridge, followed by the 12,000 men of the rearguard.

The English left behind their horses and baggage at their camp at Barmoor and marched on foot carrying only their weapons. Surrey was risking everything on fighting King James that day. The English commanders told their men that there would be no retreat. The only mounted men were about 2,000 of Lord Dacre's Borderers.

At about 11.00am the vanguard reached Twizel Bridge, it would take some time to get all the men over the narrow bridge. As I mentioned before it would have been possible for Dacre's horse to cross the Mill Ford, a mile or so upstream from Twizel.

The vanguard then marched along the track towards Cornhill, where because of the rolling hills of the area, they would be mostly out of site of any watching Scots. This track would have been a supply route to Wark castle from Berwick and Norham. If you drive along this road today it is impossible to see Flodden Hill.

On reaching Donaldson's Lodge, or Cornhill, the vanguard turned south towards Branxton, so thus the English headed towards the Scots in two columns. The vanguard would have to march about a mile south towards Branxton before it would have been possible for the Scots to see them, while the rearguard would have been mostly out of sight.

There are two views on how the two armies engaged. The first is, that it was obvious to the Scots watching towards Ford from Flodden Hill, that the English were not going to attack, and it was decided to withdraw back to Scotland by way of the fords at Coldstream. The army was marching from Flodden Hill, with Home leading, followed by the artillery, when at about 4.00 pm in the afternoon, Home came over Branxton Hill and there before him was the English army and Home immediately attacked, followed by the rest of the Scots. Although this story is possible, it is also highly unlikely. The second and most likely theory is that the Scots and English armies faced up to each other before battle commenced.

At the Scots camp on Flodden Hill on the morning of the battle, the superstitious Scots were confronted by events that gave them bad thoughts about the day ahead. Firstly the morning dew had turned the cloth of the King's tent a scarlet colour, then during a council of the noble men, a hare dashed amongst them, and despite their efforts and those of the men of the army, the hare eluded them all, only to fall dead from exhaustion at the entrance to the King's tent. It was then discovered that mice had gnawed through the leather strap of the King's helmet, and to cap it all it was a Friday. From time immorial it was considered that if anything was going to go wrong it would go wrong on a Friday, just as many people today believe that Friday 13th is unlucky.

James had not used any mounted scouts, so he new nothing of what the English were doing. At noon, the agreed time for the battle, James would have been happy that Surrey had not kept his challenge and his foes had not dared attack his mighty army.

About 1.30pm, James received word that the English had not only crossed the Till, but were now marching towards his position from the rear, and were only about three miles away.

James, wanting to verify this for himself, mounted his horse and rode off towards Branxton Hill. From here the English vanguard could be seen in glimpses as they marched towards him over the rolling hills, and once The Admiral had passed by Cramond Hill and Marledown farms near Cornhill, the English vanguard would have been in full view of the Scots King. The rearguard would have been mostly out of sight at this point.

While their King was away, the Scottish Lords held council on how they would fight the English. They all knew James was reckless in his leadership when it came to fighting.

Patrick, Lord Lyndsey of the Byres advised that the King himself should not give battle to Surrey, but marshall his army from the rear. The Lords agreed, but they overlooked one thing.

James himself!

James arrived back to be told of the plan. The King flew into a rage, threatening to hang Lord Lyndsey, shouting that they might all shame themselves by running away, yet they should never shame him by making him do the same. Despite the Scottish noblemen's fears, the King's next move was a wise one. He realised that if the English reached the top of Branxton Hill intact, Surrey would have the advantage. The Scots guns were dug in facing east and would be of no use at all, however if the Scots reached Branxton Hill first, James's mighty army would sweep the English off the hill and into Branxton Bog at the bottom. So it was ordered that the guns be taken from

The terrain that the Scots Guns were hauled over.

their positions and hauled the mile or so to Branxton Hill. As the army moved and the gunners struggled to move the guns, the camp followers set great bonfires with all the rubbish that had accumulated during the armies' stay on Flodden Hill.

On the reverse slope of Branxton Hill, which is quite flat, though pretty wet, the Scots were formed into battle order by the French adviser Di Aussi and his fifty captains.

The reverse slope of Branxton Hill where the Scots were marshalled into Battle order.

The Scots were to fight in five divisions or battles. The main weapon of the Scots were 18ft long pikes or spears, supplied by the French. Each division would advance in the shape of an arrow head or vee, with the most well protected men at the front to bear the brunt of the English archers and the initial clash with the infantry. The best protected men were of course the Lords, Earls and gentlemen, so they would be at the front of each column. This tactic worked well on flat ground, but on the steep and uneven slopes of Branxton Hill, it would prove disastrous.

For the numbers involved in the battle we have to rely on English accounts, and the way they determined how many men were in each division was purely guess work. They roughly knew what a group of five thousand men looked like, so they just doubled or trebled that figure, depending on the density of the division facing them.

The left flank of the Scots was made up of about 7,000 borderers commanded by Lord Home, and 3,000 Highlanders, mainly from Aberdeenshire led by the Earl of Huntly. The Borderers on this occasion giving up their traditional way of fighting on horseback with their short lances, to fight in the way they had been instructed by the French.

In the left centre battle, were 9,000 men from Perthshire, Angus, Forfar and Fife led by three great Scottish Earls, William Hay/Earl of Errol, John Lindsey/Earl of Crawford and William Graham/Earl of Montrose.

Next was the King's division in the right centre of the formation.

This division had as many as 15,000 men. James's household were at the front under the banners of St Andrew, St Margaret and the Royal Banner carried by Sir Adam Foreman. Around them were most of the nobility of Scotland, including the Earls of Cassillis, Morton and Rothes, Lords Herries, Maxwell, Innermeath, Borthwick and Sempill. All had their own small army of armed men from their estates. Also in this battle was the contingent from Edinburgh led by their provost and including the city band, men from Ayr, Haddington, Galloway, also the Western Lowlands.

The right flank of the army was formed by a Highland division of about 5,000 men armed with their traditional weapons, claymores, axes and bows, rather than the long pikes. Archibald Campbell, Earl of Argyle and Matthew Stewart, Earl of Lennox commanded the Highlanders.

The clans of the Campbells of Glenorchy and Louden, McLeans of Duart, MacKenzies, Grants, MacDonalds led by McIan of Ardnamurchan and Ewan MacAllan Cameron of Lochiel and his Highlanders were in this battle.

There were also about 300 men from Caithness led by William Sinclair, Earl of Caithness. Apparently these men arrived on the evening of the 8th, and Sinclair who had been at odds with James was pardoned and welcomed to the Army. His pardon was written on a drum skin as there was no parchment available.

The fifth battle, was led by Adam Hepburn, Earl of Bothwell and consisted of about 5,000 pikemen drawn from the burghs and villages of the Lothians. This division was the reserve. Di Aussi and the Frenchmen were also part of this battle.

The artillery was positioned on the highest part of Branxton Hill, between the left wing and the left centre division. As well as all these men, there must have been all the camp followers and thousands of horses on the reverse slope of Branxton Hill.

With his army thus arrayed, King James ordered the advance to the brow of Branxton Hill.

The camp followers had set all the fires by now, and the smoke from this damp rubbish blew down northwards, for a short time obscuring both armies from each other.

It was now about 3.00pm, the English vanguard had reached the gathering stone on Crookham Moor, and could see the smoke billowing from the Scottish camp fires.

The Admiral now had to make another decision. Between him and Branxton Hill lay the Pallinsburn Bog, which the Scots thought to be impassable. The Pallins Burn, takes its name from St Pallinus, who as early as year 800 AD, baptised locals in the waters. The bog was one and a half miles long and in places 250 yards wide, and stretched from behind Branxton to where the Blue Bell Inn at Crookham stands, and discharged into the River Till near Sandyford. There was only one crossing point in the middle of the bog, a small bridge known locally as the Branx Brig.

Pallinsburn Bog.

Here again historians fail to agree about how the English artillery reached the battlefield. Some say the bridge was too narrow to get the artillery across, so the guns were sent via an old road to Branxton, by way of Learmouth and Moneylaws, but neither The Admiral or the Bishop of Durham mention this in their accounts of the Battle. You can see the approaches to the bridge from Branxton Hill, but it is impossible to see the bridge itself.

The vanguard crossed the Branx Brig at about 3.30pm. Once across the Branx Brig, the first columns of the English vanguard advanced out of the small valley where the Pallins Burn now runs, to where the road is now between Branxton and the Blue Bell Inn, and then up onto the crest of the small hill on which the present day village of Branxton sits. The smoke from the Scots fires now was clearing, there in full view of the Admiral and the vanguard were the Scottish host, in battle array.

On top of the hill, Robert Borthwick immediately ordered his guns to open fire on the English.

Route of the English Vanguard.

Some of the Admiral's men panicked as the cannon balls flew over their heads, but the Admiral did not. He had advanced too far on his own, and there being no sign of his father and the rearguard. The Admiral ordered his troops back off the field, out of sight of the Scots. King James stopped Borthwick firing on the Admiral, because in some romantic notion he wanted the whole English army in front of his great army. There is no doubt that if the Scots had attacked at this moment, the outcome of the Battle of Flodden would have been different. The vanguard would have been trapped with the bog behind them.

The Admiral, aware of the danger he was in, pulled from around his neck a favour, his Agnus Dei, and sent it with a messenger to Surrey, (my Lord Howard requires my Lord (Earl) Surrey to advance his rearguard and join his right wing and left wing, as the Scots were of that might that the vanguard was not of power to counter them).

Surrey in fact, had most of his troops across the Pallins Burn at Sandyford, and was advancing towards Branxton. *'A brook of breadth of a tailors yard'*.

At about ten to four, the two columns merged and advanced in one long column, mostly hidden from the Scots, along the road that now runs behind the battle field. This road is called Dickie's Den. In the front of the English column was Sir Edmund Howard and at the rear, some way behind the Earl of Surrey, was Sir Edward Stanley.

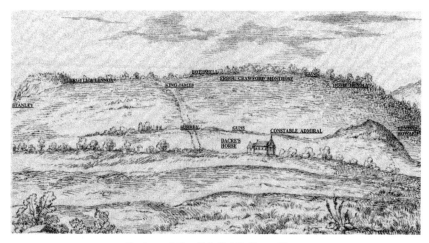

Scots and English Battle formations.

The English marched onto the battle field, when the vanguard had passed beyond the hill that the monument now stands on. This hill is known as Piperton or Pipers' Hill.

The English battle order had changed from being two divisions with two wings each, to four divisions or battles to match the Scottish Army. This decision must have been made very quickly and efficiently, having been done in the short time that the vanguard and rearguard joined. It is some evidence that Surrey's army was mostly made up of professional soldiers.

The right wing of the English army took up position in the fields to the west of Pipers' hill, towards the present day farm of Moneylaws, keeping the Oxendean Burn, which runs through this part of the battlefield, between them and the Scots.

The right wing was led by Sir Edward Howard, and with him were about 4,000 Lancashire, Cheshire and Yorkshire men, and a small number of Northumberland men, a few Howard retainers.

The right centre was positioned in front of Pipers' Hill. This battle was led by Thomas Howard, The Admiral. With him were the marines from the fleet. These men fought under the command of their ships' captains, Sir William Sidney of the ship "the Great Barque", Edward Echynham of "the Spaniard", James King of "the Julian of Dartmouth" and 12 others. In the centre of this battle and positioned near Pipers' Hill, were 2,000 men of the Bishop of Durham, these were led by Sir William Boulmer, and they carried the Sacred Banner of St. Cuthbert. There were also men from Northumberland and Durham led by Lord Ogle and Sir William Gascoigne. Also with the Admiral was old Sir Marmaduke Constable and his contingent of East Riding men.

Constable's under captains included his brother William, three of his sons, two of his cousins and his brother in law, Sir William Percy and his Northumberland men. There were about 9,000 men in all.

The left centre battle was Surrey's command. Here he had his own retainers, men from South Yorkshire led by George Darcy, Lord Scrope's men from Swaledale and Wensleydale, the citizens of York and Whitby and men who were retainers of the Bishop of Ely. In all about 7,000 men. They were positioned near to where Branxton vicarage is and the road to Branxton Hill dissects the battle field.

The Left wing consisted of 3,500 men of the Earl of Derby, led by his fifth son, Sir Edward Stanley, (his other men had been dispersed to bolster the other divisions in the English army). They were someway behind the main force, but were destined to play a vital part in the Battle of Flodden.

Lord Dacre's horse were to be used as a reserve to fight in whatever part of the field they were required. He had about 2,000 Border men including John Heron, The Bastard of Ford.

The ordinance were placed equally between the two centre divisions.

The English were armed with a double bladed weapon with a hook on the opposite side of its shaft called a billhook, axes and the dreaded English longbows. A large proportion of the English wore armour, and were better protected than their foes.

In front of the Admiral and Surrey's divisions was quite a steep slope, which ran down to a boggy ditch. This offered them some protection as the Scots would have to climb this slope to reach them. Edmund Howard's right wing did not have this natural defence in front of them.

At about 4.15pm, the Scots guns opened fire, with Sir Nicholas Appleyard returning the compliment. The English used iron cannon balls while the Scots used lead cannon balls. The English also fired small round stones, which were like a modern day cluster bomb. The history books tell that the Scots guns could not be depressed enough to hit the English Army, and that the English guns were deadly accurate in their discharge.

There is evidence that shows some of the Scots guns did find their mark.

In the early part of the 19th century, when the land around Branxton was being drained, a lead thirteen and a half pound ball was found in the west part of the bog and this must have been targeted at the English as they were marching onto the field. Two other lead balls were found in the field where Sir Edmund Howard took up his position.

Two iron balls were found around this time, both had been fired by the English guns. One was found in the side of Branxton Hill and the other behind the Scots position.

The history books also tell us that the English guns knocked out the Scots guns very quickly and killed Robert Borthwick, the master gunner. After the battle many of the Scots guns were captured and described by the English as the finest pieces they had seen. These would have been the seven brass cannon (seven sisters).

There is no doubt a 4" or 5" iron ball landing in amongst such an easy target as the massed ranks of Scots on top of the hill would have caused a lot of disruption. The artillery duel that we read about could not have lasted very long, perhaps fifteen minutes, before the Scots left wing advanced down the hill.

An old ballad describes the action:

> *"Then ordinance great anon out brast*
> *On either side with thundering thumps*
> *And roaring guns, with fire fast*
> *Then levelled out great leaden lumps"*

The Battle of Flodden was really four separate battles and each with its own outcome.

Shortly after the English took the field and the guns started firing, at approximately 4.30pm, the Scots division nearest the Scots artillery moved off. This was the 10,000 Borderers and Highlanders of Home and Huntly.

Whether they were ordered to attack or that their tight ranks had been receiving balls that were meant for the Scots guns, we do not know. Down the rain sodden hill the Borderers advanced in good order, their pikes bristling like a hedgehogs' spikes, Huntley's Highlanders, with their great swords and bows beside the Borderers.

The Border slogan rent the sky, A Home! A Gordon! Was the cry (Scotts Marmion).

Waiting to do battle with them was Sir Edmund Howard and his 4,000 men. Already outnumbered by more than two to one, this division started to waver before the Scots were half way down the hill, men started to drop their weapons and banners and started to flee. The closer the Scots got, more and more of the weak-willed English ran from the field. Again an old ballad tells this story.

> *"With whom encountered a strong Scot*
> *Which was the Kings chief chamberlain*
> *Lord Home by name, of courage hot,*
> *Who manfully marched them again.*
>
> *Ten thousand Scots, well tried and told*
> *Under his standard stout he led*
> *When the Englishmen did them behold*
> *For fear at first they would have fled"*

By the time the Scots engaged Howard, they outnumbered the English by almost twenty to one.

Home and Huntly engage Edmund Howard.

Those that were left though, fought desperately and bravely. An English Knight called Brian Tunstall of Thurland is said to have knelt down and taken a small piece of earth as a final communion, then charging into the Scots alone, he managed to kill one Highlander and wounded several others, before succoming to the advancing hoards.

All around Howard, knights fell to the Scottish pikes and Highland broadswords. The Scots slaughtered all who challenged them. These brave Englishmen could be compared to the Japanese suicide pilots of the second world war. Charging the Scots knowing that their chance of survival would have been nil. The men from Macclesfield led by Christopher Savage were all killed and their banner taken by the Border men of Selkirk. Maurice Berkley, John Bostock, Sir William Handforth, Thomas Venables, Robert Foulhurst, Robert Warkup and Sir William Fitzwilliam all died at the hands of the Borderers. Sir John Booth and John Laurence upheld the honour of Cheshire, leading what was left of their men into the unbroken pike hedgehog. Before long Edmund Howard was almost entirely on his own, save for a few retainers and his standard bearer, who was quickly beaten down and hewed to pieces.

The Borderers, always looking for a profit out of their endeavours, realised the large ransom that could be made for such an important prisoner, tried to capture Howard. Three times he was knocked to the ground, but each time he recovered and managed to fend off his would be captors.

At this time Lord Dacre's border horse came into the fight, charging into Home's Borderers. John Heron, was badly wounded as he fought his way through the Scots to reach Edmund Howard. He managed to guide Howard towards his brother's division. Stumbling and fighting a rearguard action,

Howard's path was blocked by Sir Davy Home of Wedderburn, Duns, a kinsman of Lord Home. Davy Home had seven sons, George who was killed at Flodden, David, Alexander, John, Robert, Andrew and Patrick. They were known as the seven spears of Wedderburn. Edmund Howard and Sir Davy Home engaged in hand to hand fighting in which Howard slew the Home, and then managed to reach the Admiral's division, who were now heavily engaged themselves.

Lord Dacre's Borderers clashed with Home's Borderers, and although less in numbers, they stemmed the Border tide. They killed three of Lord Home's cousins including Cuddy Home of Fast Castle, several Border gentlemen and Highland chieftains. The Scots also killed about 200 of Dacre's men, and some prisoners were taken including Dacre's brother Philip, Sir Humphrey Lysle and Sir Harry Grey, who had greeted the English Princess Margaret at Felton Bridge, on her way to her marriage over ten years before Flodden.

Before long, both sets of Borderers disengaged and withdrew, it has to be remembered that many on both sides would have known each other, some of them even related through marriage, and a Borderer was reluctant to kill another Borderer unless there was some profit in it for them.

Legend has it that both Home and Dacre agreed to withdraw, although both later denied this.

Lord Home was blamed for his inaction at the Battle of Flodden, quite wrongly I believe. My reasons for this are that Home would have driven the English back across the field, almost to Dickie's Den, perhaps even further, and from this position Home would not have seen what was happening to the rest of the Scots army. His view being obscured by the slopes of Pipers' Hill. The English accounts of the battle state that there was a strong wind blowing northwards, so there is every chance Home might not have even heard the noise of battle. Home would have seen that the rest of the Scots army had left their position on Branxton Hill and he maybe assumed that they would have the same success as he had. By the time he realised what was happening it was too late and Home, who was a skilful commander, would have decided that Scotland would have to be defended from a possible English invasion, therefore he did not commit his men to the slaughter that was taking place elsewhere that day.

The Borderers and Highlanders now withdrew towards Moneylaws Farm. Dacre stood on the ground that had been occupied by Edmund Howard and watched the Scots withdraw.

Home's Borderers took no further part in the Battle that day, although according to the late Sir Alec Douglas Home, his ancestor sent half his men to the fords at Coldstream, and the other half stood near the battle field all night and gave what help they could to the remnants of the Scottish Army. At some time, Home's men must have been back on the top of Branxton Hill to collect their horses.

When Home and Huntly advanced and engaged the English left wing, King James watched many of the English run. Now was the time to make the rest of the English run.

James, grabbing a pike, called for his household to join him at the front of his battle and charged off down Branxton Hill. It should be remembered that James was of the same line as King Robert The Bruce and had Bruce's blood running through his veins.

King James was being true to character, as described by the Spanish ambassador at Norham in 1497, and rushed off to fight without giving any commands to his other troops. Because of the contours of Branxton Hill, for King James to see Surrey's formation, his division would have been about fifty yards in front of the rest the Scots army, and would have been well down the hill before the left centre division moved off.

The Scots left centre division, led by the Earls of Errol, Crawford and Montrose advanced when they saw their King moving.

The upper part of Branxton Hill over which the left centre division advanced, has remained uncultivated for many years, and when you walk over this field in good weather it is difficult not to slip. The Scots had to descend this slope when it was wet and with a strong wind on their backs, and this did as much harm to their ranks as the English guns. Many of the Scots removed their footwear to stop themselves from slipping on the steep slope. When in range the English bowmen let off their deadly rain into the advancing Scots, and the English guns would still be firing at this stage. Despite the arrows and cannon balls the Scots columns came on.

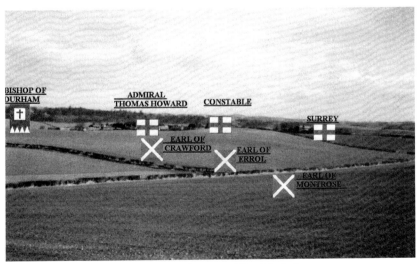

The three Earls engage The Admiral.

On reaching the bottom of the hill, the Scots found they had to cross the marshy stream, which had a concertina effect on the three Earls' division. Instead of the momentum of a massed assault like that of Home and Huntly, this division found themselves engaging the Admiral's waiting men armed with billhooks, in hundreds rather than thousands. The Scots, trying to reach the St Cuthbert's Banner on Pipers' Hill were cut to pieces by the professional English soldiers and marines. There was terrible slaughter here. It would be doubtful if any Scot got within one hundred yards of the Bishop of Durham on Pipers' Hill.

It was said that the Admiral shouted for the King of Scots to show himself and fight, but as James had his hands full elsewhere, it was the Earl of Crawford who engaged the Admiral. Both armed with axes, it was the Admiral who struck the mortal blow. The Scots advance was slowed even more by the dead of their countrymen. Montrose was one of the first casualties and the Earl of Errol died with eighty seven of his clan Hay dead around their leader.

As the English held their ground, the Scots, confused and disheartened, began to withdraw and eventually ran from the field. If Home and Huntly had destroyed the English right wing, The Admiral had gained revenge with interest.

The 15,000 men of the King's division encountered the same problems as that of the three Earls at the foot of Branxton Hill. It must have been a frightening sight for Surrey's 7,000 men, these 15,000 Scots advancing on them, and even though the boggy ground slowed the advance, the Scots hit the front of Surrey's men with such force that they pushed them back towards Branxton village. But eventually the English stood their ground and the billmen inflicting

King James engages Surrey.

terrible wounds on the Scots nobility who formed the front ranks, their pikes being chopped, they were forced to fight with their swords. These were no match for the English bills, being used in a scything motion, slicing and maiming all in front of them. The Bishop of Durham wrote that they were so mighty, large, strong and great men that they would not fall when four or five bills struck on one of them at once. This would only apply to the Lords and gentlemen who had body armour, the commoners would have fell with fewer blows. Lords Maxwell and Herries were amongst the first to fall. James leading by example, charged the English line, killing five before he was forced to draw his sword. James was trying to reach Surrey, who was commanding his men from his carriage. The King's path was blocked by a young knight called Richard Harbottle. James took his sword and dealt such a mighty blow that it cleft Harbottle from his neck almost to his waist. It is said that James got to within a few feet of Surrey before he fell. The Earl of Surrey was protected by several of his personal soldiers, and it was one of these who killed the King of Scots. James was hit by an arrow that went through his mouth and out through the back of his head. An English bill also came down and almost severed his left hand, and a final blow made sure of the King's demise, slicing across his throat. James died almost unnoticed by the majority of his division, that had now spread out across the field and were now engaging the Admiral's men who had swung round and were attacking the King's divisions flank, it was probably at this time that Bothwell and the Scots reserve entered the fight. The King's banner was eventually cast to the ground when Sir Adam Foreman was killed not far from the King.

Stanley routes the Highland division.

What of the Scots fourth battle, the right wing of Highlanders commanded by the Earls of Lennox and Argyle? They had watched the two centre divisions and the reserves join battle with the English. Why they waited to join the battle is a mystery. It could have been because they received no orders from the King, or they were late in arriving from the camp, we shall never know.

Sir Edward Stanley however, commanding the English left, found and engaged them on the top of the hill, and in doing so probably saved the English army from defeat.

Stanley ordered his men to climb up Pate Hill in Crookham Dean, to the west of Marden. This ground was hidden from the top so the Highlanders would not have known what hit them. Stanley's archers got right behind the Scots, with the Stanley's men at arms on the Highlander's right flank. At the time the archers loosed their arrows the Scots were preparing to charge down the hill. The first wave of arrows hit the unprotected backs of the Scots, and as they turned to see where the attack came from, the second wave of arrows hit their target. At the same time the English, in three companies, led by Sir William Molyneux, charged the now confused Scots. Lennox, Argyle and Caithness, Lord Darnley and the clan chiefs Campbell and McIan died trying to rally their Highlanders. Many Highlanders shocked by the surprise attack ran down the hill. Those that were left were cut to pieces by the English. It was said there were rivers of blood running down Branxton Hill. Stanley's men gave chase after the Highlanders, across the battle field they ran, stumbling over the countless dead bodies. Stanley's men stopped the chase, and joined in the main battle still raging on, this way and that way over the field.

King James's Division completly overwhelmed.

Why did Stanley climb up the hill to engage the Scots right wing? I believe that for some reason Stanley was well behind the main body of the English Army, and he was following the original plan of climbing Branxton Hill and engaging the Scots at Flodden Hill. On reaching the top of Pate Hill, Stanley discovered that the only Scots left were the Highland division, ready to charge down the Branxton Hill.

The remnants of James's army fought on desperately, although now almost surrounded.

> *Though billmen ply their ghastly blow,*
> *Unbroken was the ring,*
> *The stubborn spearmen still made good,*
> *Each stepping where his comrade stood,*
> *The instant that he fell.*
>
> *(Scotts Marmion)*

Around the King's body lay his own natural son, the Bishop of St Andrews, The Earls of Bothwell, Cassillis and Morton. Some of who were left tried to surrender, but Surrey's men cut them down with so much vengeance and cruelty. There would be headless and limbless bodies, men dying from their terrible wounds, some men would have been trampled to death. Only about four hundred Scots were taken prisoner, including two of James's household, but nobody of great importance.

The Earl of Huntly who was with Lord Home in the Scots left wing must have re-entered the Battle, as his standard was captured during the battle by Sir William Molyneux who had led the English charge against the Scots right wing on the top of Branxton Hill.

Surrey ordered his troops to withdraw when darkness stopped the slaughter on both sides, but he was unclear who was the victor. Surrey gathered his commanders and gave them a tongue lashing for not winning the day. The fight lasted between two and three hours. It has to be remembered that in 1513 a different calendar was used, and this would put the 9th of September 1513 around the 5th of October in our calendar. Add to that it was a grey wet afternoon, the darkening would close in quicker. The Lord Admiral wrote that some English chased the Scots about three leagues towards the Border, the chase ending in another fight that left the English with 200 dead, Scots casualties are not known. Throughout the night, the English men claimed their spoils from the dead and dying. English archers would put their own mark on their arrows, so being able to identify their own victims and claim their belongings as booty. Whether the archers were allowed to do this at Flodden or it was just a free for all, we do not know.

The wounded and dying were placed in Branxton Church, and Thomas Godergyl, the Vicar of Branxton would have been very busy tending to these unfortunate souls.

In the morning, it became clear to the English commanders that they had taken part in a terrible fight and inflicted heavy damage to the Scots army. Thousands of the dead had been despoiled, there were great piles of naked bodies littered all around the blood red ground, the rest of leaderless Scots army had melted away from the field.

Tweeds echoes heard the ceaseless plash
As many a broken band
Disordered through her current dash
To gain the Scottish land

(Scotts Marmion)

The exact numbers of dead on either side is difficult to know nearly 500 years on, and we have to rely on the English accounts, which state that at least 10,000, possibly more Scots died, and about 1,500 English dead, although the information board at the Flodden Memorial gives the total as 4,000 and is probably nearer to the mark.

KNOWN BURIAL PITS

To give a comparison, at the Battle of Waterloo, there were 20,000 killed in about five hours of fighting, an average of one dead soldier every ninety seconds. At the Battle of Flodden someone was killed on average every seventy seven seconds.

The Lord Admiral and Lord Dacre were inspecting the Scots guns, on top of Branxton Hill, when a large number of Scots horsemen appeared near Moneylaws, to the west of the Battlefield. The English fired off a few shots, and the Scots withdrew. These horseman were presumably Borderers of Lord Home.

The English found a large amount of booty upon the reverse slope of Branxton Hill. The Bishop of Durham wrote *"Would not have believed that their beer was so good, had it not been tasted and viewed by our folks to their great refreshing."* Obviously the Scots had hoped to collect this after their victory. It is possible the Scots horsemen that appeared that morning were going to help themselves to all the plunder.

By mid morning King James's bloodied body was found and pulled from the piles of mutilated bodies. His body was identified by Lord Dacre who knew him well, he had often played cards with the monarch. A captured member of James's household, Sir William Scott, also confirmed that it was the King. King James IV can be added to an amazing statistic, that of all the Monarchs that ruled Scotland up to the union of the crowns, only two died in their beds.

On realising his victory, Surrey gathered his army around Pipers' Hill, and the Bishop of Durham held a service thanking God for their great victory. Surrey then knighted many of his captains.

For his success, a grateful King Henry, bestowed on the Earl of Surrey, the title of Duke of Norfolk. A title the family still hold to this day.

The English "Borderers" lived up to their reiver reputation by driving off some of the oxen that had pulled the English guns, they then raided the English camp at Barmoor, killing those that had been left to guard it, stealing some of the thousands of horses and whatever else they could carry. The Bishop of Durham wrote that the *"Borderers did more harm to our army than the Scots, they even captured members of the English army and gave them over to Home's Borderers as prisoners!"*

Branxton Church.

King James's body was laid in the church at Branxton, before it was taken to Berwick to be embalmed. His body was firstly disembowelled, then covered in leather sewn tightly, and finally encased in lead, with joints being soldered. There is an entry in the exchequer accounts of money paid to the English army for the body of King James being embalmed and carried to Windsor.

Also payed for dyverse costes charges and expenens had and susteyned aswell in serying ledyng and sawdrying of the dede course of the kyng of Scottes, as also in carrying and conveying hym to York and so forth to Wyndsore as in the seid boke of parcelles and a bill signed lord Leiftenaunt apon this declaracion examyned it may appere. Fourteen pounds, nine shillings and ten pence.

From Berwick the body was carried to Newcastle, where it was laid in a lead casket for transportation to London. On reaching London, King Henry's Queen, Katherine, was going to have James's head sent to her husband in France, but sent his bloody sur coat instead. She wrote to Henry *"your grace will see how I can keep my promys, sending you for your banners a Kings coat. I thought to send himself unto you, but our Englishmen's hearts would not suffer it."*

The body was then taken to Sheen monastery in Surrey, where it remained unburied for many years, although King Henry wrote to the Pope on October 13, asking him to write to the Bishop of London to allow the body of the King of Scots, who died under excommunication, to be carried to London and buried with royal honours at St Paul's. The Pope gave his permission, but James never received a burial with royal honours. It was not until the reign of Elizabeth the First that James was finally laid to rest. Lancelot Young, master glacier to the Queen, on seeing workman using James's head as a football. The head, because it had been embalmed, still had hair on its scalp and a full red beard.

Lancelot Young took the head to his home in London, and kept it for its sweet fragrance and for the entertainment of his guests. James's head was eventually buried in an unmarked grave in St Michael's Church in Wood Street, London, along with various other bones from the chancel of the church. The church has long been replaced by an office block, though there is no mention of remains being taken from this site.

Along with the King, most of Scotland's ruling class died at Branxton. Amongst the dead were an Archbishop, a bishop, two abbots, ten Earls, nineteen Lords, as well as hundreds of knights and gentlemen, of which many came from the Borders. It was said that not a household in the south of Scotland was left untouched by Flodden.

> *Scotia felt thine ire o'Odin*
> *On the bloody fields o'Flodden,*
> *Where oor faither's fell wi' honour*
> *Roond oor King and countries banner.*
> (*song sung at Hawick Common Riding*)

The Earl of Caithness and all his men were killed, and it was declared bad luck to cross the river Ord north of Inverness on a Monday, the same day of the week that the Caithness men had crossed the river on their way to the Borders.

The Frenchmen who had been advisors to the Scots, had fought in the battle and were blamed for the defeat, those that survived the English longbow and billhook, perished on the end of a Scots sword or lance. Most of the dead were buried where they fell, presumably by the captured Scots and the English victors. Two burial pits are in the west of the field where Home and Huntly had fought, close to Dickie's Den, and are marked on earlier maps of the area. It was said that the Oxendean Burn ran red for three days after the battle.

The water supply for Pallinsburn House comes from a tank on the west of Branxton Hill, and when it was installed in the nineteenth century, the contractors dug the water track through the middle of the battlefield. They came across countless bones of the buried from one side of the battlefield to the other. Many skeletons were found just outside the church door when the path was widened in the middle of the nineteenth century. These remains were re-interred in the left hand corner of the church yard. There is also a spot known to the locals as the Sodger's Grave. It lies at the side of the metal road close to Moneylaws Farm road end, and supposedly contains the body of a poor soul who died of his wounds while leaving the field during the night after the battle.

There is also a burial pit near the farm of West Learmouth. This pit was found about thirty years ago by a digger driver who was draining a field and dug up a large quantity of human bones. They were only two to three feet under the ground. The position of this pit would confirm what the Lord Admiral wrote, that the English chased the Scots for three leagues towards the Border. This burial pit lies about three quarters of a mile from the battlefield, and is in a direct line with the ford in the River Tweed at Coldstream.

Tradition also tell of some bodies being taken by the Nuns of Coldstream Priory from the battlefield, back to the Priory to be buried in consecrated ground, and when foundations were being dug for the houses that now stand where the Priory was, a large number of bones were found.

It is also said that bodies of the fallen were taken to Yetholm Church, about seven miles from the battlefield. Many families also took their kinsmen home with them. The Spears of Wedderburn wrapped the bodies of their father and brother in their banner and carried them home to be buried in the family plot. Part of the green and white Home saltire banner is still in existence. As Wedderburn is not far from the village of Swinton, it is probable that the bell on the church was rung for Davy and George Home.

Many Scots, unable to believe that their beloved King had been killed, claimed that the body the English took from the field was not that of James, because the iron chain belt James wore was never produced as evidence, and apparently several gentlemen were dressed almost identical to the King. It was also widely believed that James had been carried from the field by four noble men before going to the Holy Land.

Lord Home was accused by James Stewart, Earl of Moray, of taking the King from the battlefield and murdering him at Hume Castle. During the building of the present structure at Hume a skeleton, wrapped in animal skin and iron chains, was pulled from an old well. Could this have been King James?

When word reached Edinburgh of the death of the King and the defeat of the army, a wall was hastily erected round the city. Small fragments of the Flodden Wall can still be seen today in the St Leonard's and St Mary's area of the city.

Flodden Wall.

Lord Dacre was ordered to raid and plunder the Borders at his pleasure and this he did, but he nearly came unstuck when he and his brother crossed the Border on the 10th of November. Dacre's force was caught by David Ker of Ferniehurst and a large party of Scots near Ruecastle. Dacre retreated to Scatler Ford, where he was saved by the timely arrival of his brother, who must have been released by his Scots captors shortly after Flodden. Lord Home then joined Ker and led a counter raid. If nothing else, this proved to the English that Flodden was not as a complete defeat as they thought it was. Although Dacre devastated the Border land the following spring.

Lord Home, who as Chief Justice south of the Forth, negotiated a peace treaty with the English. As Scotland now only had an infant to succeed to the throne, Lord Home proposed the Duke of Albany as regent. But things did not work out the way Home had planned, he later took up arms against the regent. Home was seen as a powerful threat to Albany and the government of Scotland.

In 1515 Albany destroyed Hume Castle, and in 1516, Alexander 3rd Lord Home along with his brother were executed for treason. Home was also charged for his part in the defeat at Flodden, and for murdering the King.

In Home's place as Warden of the Marches, the regent Albany installed a Frenchman, Anthony Darcy, the Sieur de La Bastie. The Homes confronted Darcy near the Home castle of Broomhouse, Duns, and accused him of being involved in the death of their Lord. They chased the unfortunate Frenchman and caught him when his horse floundered in a bog. The Homes cut off his head, then tied it to one of their saddles and paraded the head through the town of Duns as a warning to the Scottish establishment.

The Sieur de La Bastie monument stands outside of the gates of Broomhouse, and there is a small grave stone at Wedderburn Castle, home of the Spears of Wedderburn, said to be the burial place of de La Bastie's head.

There are two stories of what happened to John Heron. One that he died in the battle of Flodden, the other that Heron recovered from his wounds and a few years after Flodden, he was again taking on a Scots force. The story goes that the Scots fled the fight after losing two hundred dead to the English. Heron, desperate to satisfy his lust for killing Scotsmen chased the fleeing Scots on his own. The Scots suddenly turned on Heron, caught and killed him, claiming that it was worth two hundred of their countrymen dead to have slain John Heron, the Bastard of Ford.

King James's widow Margaret and her infant son, who would become James V, looked for sanctuary in Berwick but were turned away. They made their way up Tweedside to Coldstream, where they were welcomed by Prioress Isabella Hoppringle at Coldstream Priory. In 1542 Coldstream Priory was burned by 1,000 Englishmen, of which the 3rd Duke of Norfolk, The Admiral, who fought at Flodden was involved. The English took 2,000 marks worth of corn, captured sixty men and sixty horses. The Priory was burned again in 1545 along with many other great buildings in the Borders by the Earl of Hertford.

The church at Lennel, on the outskirts of Coldstream, is called St Mary's and All Souls after the Coldstream priory and the dead of Flodden Field.

Sieur de La Bastie Monument.

FLODDEN REMEMBERED

Flodden Memorial being unveiled.

On the 27th of September 1910, at 2.30pm in the afternoon, the Flodden Monument was unveiled by Sir George Douglas Bart. The monument was described as a 12 foot high Celtic Monolith Cross of grey Aberdeen granite, the arms of the cross were 3 feet 9 inches across, and the structure was raised on a 6 feet rustic base of rough-hewn granite blocks. It was built from funds provided by both Scots and English members of The Berwickshire Naturalists Club.

At the end of his address in front of over a thousand onlookers, Sir George Douglas told his audience *"But, from the impending and over brooding gloom there still emerge, like stars by night to solace and inspire courage, devotion, patriotic fire, doomed to extinction in their mortal part, but in their essence and effect undying! These we salute and commemorate, wherever they are found, without regard to party or nationality, to victory or defeat, to rank or to the want of it. The brave, the good, are of one rank, and to that rank we proudly bow........*

Now let this cross thus stand and thus endure, an alter of the awful God of battles; a token of remembrance wet with tears; an offering to the Manes of the slain! And let it speak to thoughtful minds in days to come, telling of ancient agony long since assuaged, of ancient feud for ever reconciled!"

Many of those who witnessed this historic occasion, would go on to fight their own Floddens, four years later in the Great War, and there would be thousands more memorials wet with tears.

Fletcher memorial, Selkirk.

During the summer, from June till August, each of the Border towns hold their festivals or Common Ridings. There are three festivals that commemorate events from the Battle. At Selkirk Common Riding, they remember Fletcher who supposedly was the sole survivor of the party that had left the town to fight for their King, and who brought back the captured Macclesfield Flag. 'The flag is cast' in the market square to bring the Common Riding to a close.

1514 Memorial, Hawick.

At Hawick Common Riding, a defeat of an English raiding party from Hexham in 1514, at a place just outside Hawick called Hornshole is celebrated. All the Hawick men had been killed at Flodden, and all that were left to defend the town were the youths. They attacked and slaughtered the invaders, taking the English flag. In Hexham can be found a Hawick banner which the good people of Hawick gave to the town of Hexham.

At Coldstream Civic Week, the brave of both nations are remembered, when a mounted cavalcade leaves the town for Branxton led by a young man who carries the Town Banner. The 'Coldstreamer' as he is known, is charged by the Earl of Home to lead the cavalcade assembled in Coldstream, to Flodden Field as his ancestors did in 1513. The 'Coldstreamer' also carries the "Home colours", presented to him by the Countess of Home. On arriving at the

Flodden Memorial the Coldstream Burgh Standard is lowered as a mark of respect to the fallen, and a wreath laid.

> *The piper plays a lament sae sad,*
> *Above the boggy Palinsburn'*
> *Where both nations men,*
> *There they lie,*
> *And in peace we will return.*
>
> (song sung at Coldstream Civic Week)

There is then a service on Branxton Hill, when a guest speaker delivers an oration on the battle. In recent years the Earl of Arundel (Surrey), accompanied by his father, the Duke of Norfolk, followed a few years later by the Earl of Home, have spoken at Flodden.

To commemorate the actions of the Nuns of Coldstream a turf is cut from Branxton Hill and wrapped in a Scottish Saltire, carried back to Coldstream on horseback. The turf is then reverently laid near to where Coldstream Priory stood, in the shadow of the graves of the Flodden heroes that are buried in Coldstream.

The very first Coldstream Flodden Cavalcade in 1952 caused quite a sensation in the press on both sides of the Border. The cavalcade of over one hundred horsemen was piped over the Tweed Bridge by Alistair Scott, to the tune of Blue Bonnets Over The Border. On reaching Branxton the horses were left tethered, while the riders marched in procession along Dickie's Den to the Memorial. The service of remembrance was held at the Flodden Memorial, with the proceedings being relayed by loud speaker to the thousands who had gathered in Dickie's Den below. At each corner of the Memorial stood a youth dressed in period chain mail and surcoats, two from England and two from Scotland

Captain J.C. Collingwood from Cornhill, who owned the land that the Memorial stands on, welcomed "our friends from the Borders".

There was a speaker for the English, Lord Lambton M.P. for Berwick, and Lord Strathden and Campbell for the Scots, and while Lord Lambton was giving his oration, Wendy Wood a well known Scottish Nationalist interrupted the speaker. She shouted through a loud hailer that Berwick was Scottish, and shame on you.

At the end of the English and Scottish orations, the Last Post was sounded and only the heavy rain which was falling broke the silence. The Provost of Coldstream, N.D.Henderson, then laid a wreath of carnations in the form of a Union Jack at the base of the memorial. Coldstream Town Councillor, Alan Leishman, who was a leading light in the founding Coldstream Civic Week, promising support to 'our new Queen', led the gathering in God Save the Queen. Wendy Wood then started singing Scots Wha Hae wi Wallace Bled.

In 1976, I had the honour of being elected Coldstreamer, and for me the emotion of laying a wreath at the Flodden Memorial is one I will carry to my grave. Every time I go to the memorial, I cannot help but think of the carnage that took place here, and for what. If King James had won the battle, would King Henry not have brought the whole might of England north and devastated Scotland. If this had happened, would France have invaded the south of England in support of Scotland? I doubt it!

Scotland and its people would have suffered which ever way the Battle of Flodden had went.

The battle has often been described as a disaster for the Scots. Well it was, but not because the Scots fought so badly, the battle was really a close run fight, Surrey only claimed victory the following day when the leaderless remains of the Scots army had left the field. The Battle of Flodden was a disaster for Scotland because of the nobility of the men who died in it.

No Scot should feel bitter about what happened at Branxton, because unlike William Wallace at Stirling Bridge and Robert the Bruce at Bannockburn, King James IV and his army were the aggressors at Flodden.

THE 1513 FLODDEN CLUB

In 1997, myself and 3 worthies decided that on the evening of the 9th of September at around 6.30pm, we would go to the Battlefield to remember the Scots who died there. So after meeting in a local pub we set off to Flodden. A short oration was delivered and two toasts. One to the King and the other to the Border men who fell. A lament was played and then we trooped back down to the car park with a feeling of what we had just done was something we should make an annual event. Back in the pub in Coldstream, and with a few whiskies under our belts, we decided to form a club, The 1513 club. Coldstream being what it is, the news of what we had done spread like wild fire, and it was amazing how our numbers quickly grew. The next year about ten of us went to the memorial on the 9th September And the following year a dinner was also held. With the club membership set a 50, there is now a waiting list to join. The next project for the 1513 club is to erect a memorial in Coldstream to Abbess Hoppringle near to the site of Coldstream Abbey. The club web site is www.Flodden1513club.com and I would welcome any comments you have about this book or about Flodden. You can send these to james@bell26.fsnet.co.uk

THE SWORD, DAGGER AND RING OF
KING JAMES IV

There is a real mystery concerning the sword and dagger of King James and the ring that Queen Anne of France sent to James. The Bishop of Durham wrote to Wolsley in London on the 20th September 1513, eleven days after the battle, informing him that *'Surrey was on his way to York with the King of Scot's body, but Surrey would not be persuaded to leave it at Durham where my folks have brought the Royal Standard of Scotland and his sword.'*

An entry on the Minutes of Chapter of the College of Arms, London, on the 3rd day of November, 1681, referring to these articles, states that his Grace the then Duke of Norfolk had been pleased to deliver to the College of Heralds "the very sword and dagger, and a gold ring set with turquoise stone, which his ancestor, Thomas Duke of Norfolk, took from James the Fourth, King of Scotland, at the battle of Flodden Field, where the said king was slain." In their custody the sword, dagger and ring have remained ever since.

Sword kept in the College of Arms, City of London, by permission of the Duke of Norfolk.

The Royal Armoury in the Tower of London has inspected the sword , but date it to fifty years after Flodden! The sword, dagger and ring were also exhibited by the College in 1934, and at that time the sword and dagger were also dated after Flodden. I wrote to the Royal Armoury in Leeds, inquiring about Maestro Domingo, whose name is inscribed on one side of the sword, and although he is mentioned in a book as being a famous sword maker, the experts in the Leeds Royal Armoury have never come across him before. Which is all a bit strange. The Leeds Royal Armoury also dated a scanned photograph of King James's sword for me, although I did not tell them that it was thought to be King James's sword. They dated the hilt late sixteenth century, and the blade possibly later. The hilt on the sword in the College of Arms was slack, so this could point to the hilt being from a different sword than the blade. All very confusing!

Please remember that King James was presented with a sword by the Spanish ambassador to the Scottish court as a gift from the King and Queen of Spain shortly after James came to the throne. The sword in London has its maker's name 'Maestro Domingo' on the blade, the sword and dagger also have matching Falcons head on the hilt. There is also an inscription on the blade which when translated reads 'Hope is Comfort for the Warrior'.

In Ford castle, are displayed replicas of King James's sword, dagger and the ring that the Queen of France sent to James and effectively caused the conflict at Branxton. These "replicas" were supposed to have been made about the year 1700 and are so well made it would be difficult to tell them from the originals, apart from the fact that they are in pristine condition and the ones in the College of Arms certainly look older and are lighter in weight than the ones at Ford.

Having seen both sets of relics, the Ford sword and dagger are identical in every detail except that one of the quiliens on the London sword has been broken off at some stage. The dagger though, is very similar to a dagger in the Museum of Border Arms and Armour, in Teviotdale. The museum state that their dagger dates from the early sixteenth century, and is a rare example of a Lowland Scots left handed sword.

This asks the question, why would someone have gone to the trouble and no doubt considerable expense to have replicas made? As I said I was fortunate to be allowed to see and handle the sword and dagger in London, and the College of Arms archivist was very surprised when I gave him photographs of the Ford items. He explained that as far as anyone knew, there is no record of their sword and dagger ever leaving the College, as they would have done to have such perfect copies made. So according to the information from the College, the Ford sword, dagger and ring would have had to have been made before 1688.

I have tried to find out when the Duke of Norfolk came into possession of the sword from Durham. The archivist at Arundel castle, the home of the Duke of Norfolk, wrote that the items that are in the College of Arms were in the Duke of Norfolk's collection in the early seventeenth century.

I have also tried to find out when the Ford sword was made and when it came to the castle. Unfortunately there is no record of this.

I received from Mr Roger Norris, the Deputy Chapter Librarian at Durham Cathedral, a page from a book called the Rites of Durham. It tells of a shrine in the cathedral in which the Royal Standard of Scotland hung alongside the St Cuthbert's banner, until the suppression of the monastic house in 1539/40. At this time the two banners were defaced and relics of the noblemen of Scotland taken from Flodden were spoiled with the intent that there should be no remembrance left within the Monastic Church of Durham. Unfortunately the relics are not mentioned individually, so we do not know for certain if King James's sword was still there at the time.

So where is King James's sword? Is the real one in London? How did the English know that the sword they had in 1513 was King James's? The Bishop of Durham wrote *"the English did not trouble themselves with prisoners, but slew and stripped King, bishop, lords and nobles, and left them naked on the field.*

The ring in the College of Arms has never been dated either, even though the college is not far from Goldsmiths Hall in the City of London, whose experts I am sure would only be to glad to help. We shall never know the answers until the London relics are date tested, even then we might not know the truth.

Over the years there have been many items found on the battlefield, including a gold and sapphire ring which was found in 1818. The style of this ring is known as a Bishop's ring, although this does not guarantee that a Bishop wore the ring. Again I have been fortunate to examine and handle this ring. The ring was bought in a collection by the British Museum from a Dr Mantell in 1853. The sapphire is an unpolished stone, and although I know nothing about valuable stones I was certainly impressed with this one.

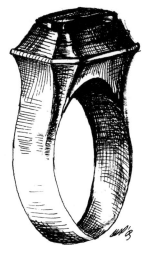

Bishops ring. Illustration by Michelle Payne.

The British Museum date the ring to the 12th or 13th century, but when asked, would not give a valuation. Given the date of the ring, there is no doubt in my mind that it would have been worn by someone of importance at the battle, maybe even King James's son the Bishop of St Andrews.

There was a sword also found when the bog at the bottom of the field was being drained, unfortunately it fell onto the ground and being so fragile after being buried for all these years, the sword broke into a thousand pieces.

I will now pull a veil over the last great medieval battle to be fought on English soil. Flodden, where the bright light of Scotland was extinguished, never to shine again.

In the years that followed Flodden, the cannon would become more accurate and deadly, the billhooks and longbows, that inflicted so much damage to the Scots would be replaced by pistols and muskets with bayonets.

I have discovered over the years that, almost every one who is interested or read about the Battle of Flodden have their own views as to what happened at Branxton, but whatever your thoughts are on the Battle of Flodden, none of us should ever forget the sacrifice that the men of both Scotland and England made on the bloody fields of Branxton Moor.

> *'Beside Branxton, in a brook,*
> *Breathless they lie,*
> *Gaping against the moon;*
> *Their ghosts went away.'*

SCOTTISH MEN OF RANK WHO FELL AT FLODDEN

The following is a list of the Royal household of Scotland and men of rank who fell during the battle. The list contains most of the noblemen who died but there may have been others. The commoners who died in their thousands do not have any recognition.

King James IV
Alexander Stewart, Archbishop of St Andrews, Chancellor of Scotland, natural son of James IV
George Hepburn, Bishop of the Isles
Laurence Oliphant, Abbot of Inchaffrey
William Bunch, Abbot of Kilwinning
Thomas Dickson, Dean of Restalrig.
Archibold Campbell, 2nd Earl of Argylle
John Douglas, 2nd Earl of Morton
William Graham, 1st Earl of Montrose
William Hay, 4th Earl of Errol
Adam Hepburn, 2nd Earl of Bothwell
David Kennedy, 1st Earl of Cassillis
John Lindsay, 2nd Earl of Crawford
William Sinclair, 2nd Earl of Caithness
John Stewart, 2nd Earl of Athol
William Leslie, 3rd Earl of Rothes
Mathew Stewart, 2nd Earl of Lennox, Constable of Scotland
James Stewart, Earl of Buchan, 2nd son of James IV
Andrew Stewart, Lord Avandale
William Borthwick, Lord Borthwick.
Robert Crichton, Lord Crichton of Sanquhar
Alexander Elphinstone, Lord Elphinstone
Robert Erskine, Lord Erskine
John Forbes, Lord Forbes
John Hay, Lord Hay of Yester
Andrew Herries, Lord Herries of Terreagles
James Ogilvy, Lord Ogilvy of Airlie
Thomas Stewart, Lord Innermeath
John Maxwell, Lord Maxwell

John Ross, Lord Ross of Halkhead
John Semple, Lord Semple
George Seton, Lord Seton
Henry Sinclair, Lord Sinclair
Robert Kieth, Lord Kieth
Fraser, Lord Lovat
James Abercromby of Birkenbog
John Adam
Andrew Anstruther of Anstruther
Robert Arnot of Woodmill
John Balfour of Denmill
Robert Blackadder of Blackadder
Sir Alexander Boswell of Balmuto
Thomas Boswell of Auchinleck
Three brothers surname Broomfield, from Berwickshire
Alan Cathcart, Master of Cathcart
Robert Cathcart
John Cathcart
Sir Duncan Campbell of Glenorchy
John de Carnegy of Kinnaird
Robert Colvill of Hilton
John Cornwal of Bonhard
John Crawford of Ardagh
Robert Crawford of Auchinames
John Crawford of Crawfordlands
George Douglas, Master of Angus
Sir William Douglas of Glenbervie
Sir John Douglas
Sir William Douglas of Drumlanrig
Sir John Dunbar of Mochrum
Robert Dickson of Buchtrig
William Fleming of Barochen
Sir Adam Foreman, Standard Bearer to King James IV
Thomas Frazer, Master of Lovat
Sir William Gordon
Sir Alexander Gordon of Lochinvar
John Grant
Robert Gray of Litfie

Archibold Graham of Garvock
George Graham of Calandar
Sir Alexander Guthrie of Guthrie
William Haig, Baron of Bemerside
Adam Hall
Sir John Haldane of Gleneagles
Sir Adam Hepburn of Craigs
James Henderson of Fordell
David HopPringle of Smailholm
Sir Patrick Houston of Houston
Sir Davy Home of Wedderburn
Cuthbert Home of Fast Castle
William Johnston of Johnston
William Keith
Sir John Keith of Ludquahairn
John Keith of Craig
Sir John Lauder of Halton
Sir Alexander Lauder of Blyth
James Lauder
Sir Robert Livingston of Easterweems
William Livingston
William Lesley
Walter Lindsay
David Lindsay
Allan Lockhart of Cleghorn
Sir John Macfarlane of Macfarlane
Hector Maclean of Dowart
Sir William Maclellan of Bomby
Sir Alexander Macnaughton of Macnaughton
Sir Thomas Maule of Panmure
William Maitland of Leithington and Thirlestane
Sir John Melville of Raith
John Melvill of Carnbee
Cuthbert Montgomery of Skelmorly
Sir Malcolm McKeene
Andrew Moray of Abercairny and Ogilvy
George Moray
Patrick Murray of Ochtertyre

John Murray of Falahill
John Murray of Blackbarony
Sir Alexander Napier
Colin Oliphant
Alexander Ogilvy
Andrew Pitcairn
Sir Alexander Ramsay of Dalhousie
William, eldest son of Sir William de Ruthven
Sir Alexander Scott of Hassendean
Sir Alexander Seton of Touch
Sir William Sinclair of Roslin
Sir John Stewart of Minto
Sir John Somerville of Quathquan
Alexander Skene of Skene
William Spotswood of Spotswood
Sir John Stewart of Garlies
Sir David Wemyss
Elliot of Redheugh
Sir John Home, Sunlaws

ENGLISH MEN OF RANK WHO FELL AT FLODDEN

Again the following list is probably incomplete.

Sir John Booth
Sir William Fitzwilliam
Sir William Handforth
Sir Richard Harbottle
Sir Bryan Tunstall
Maurice Berkley
John Bostock
Robert Foulhurst
John Lawrence
Christopher Savage
Thomas Venables
Robert Warkup

BALLADS, SONGS AND POEMS ABOUT THE BATTLE OF FLODDEN

The Flowers of the Forest

I've heard the liltin' at our ewe-milkin'
Lasses a-liltin' before dawn o'day ;
Now there's a moanin' on ilka green loanin',
The flowers of the forest are a' wede away.

At buchts in the mornin', nae blyth lads are scornin',
Lasses are lanely, and dowie, ans wae;
Nae daffin, nae gabbin, but sighin' and sbbin',
Ilk ane lifts her leglin and hies her away.

In har'st at the shearin', nae youths now are jeerin',
The bandsters are runkled, and lyart, and gray;
At fair or at preachin', nae wooin', nae fleechin',
The flowers of the forest, are a' wede away.

At e'en, in the gloamin', nae swankies are roamin',
'Bout stackc, 'mang the lasses at bogle to play;
But each ane sits dreary, lamentin' her dearie,
The flowers of the forest are a' wede away.

Dool and wae for the order sent our lads tae the border,
The English for ance by guile won the day;
The flowers of the forest, that fought aye the foremost,
The prime o' our land lie cauld in the clay.

We'll hear nae mair liltin' at our ewe-milkin',
Women and bairns are dowie and wae;
Sighin' and moanin' on ilka green loanin',
The flowers of the forest are a' wede away.

Flodden Field

King Jamie hath made a vow,
Keepe it well if he may!
That he will be at lovely London
Upon Saint James, his day.

'Upon Saint James his day at noone,
At faire London will I be,
And all the lords in merrie Scotland,
They shall dine there with me.

Then bespake good Queene Margaret,
The teares fell from her eye:
'Leave off these warres, most noble king,
Keep your fidelitie.

'The water runnes swift and wondrous deepe,
From bottome unto brimme;
My brother henry hath men good enough;
England is hard to winne'.

'Away quoth he, 'with this silly foole!
In prison fast let her lie;
For she is come of the English bloud,
And for these words she shall dye'.

With that bespake Lord Thomas Howard,
The queenes chamberlaine that day;
'If that you put Queene Margaret to death,
Scotland shall rue it alway'.

Then a rage King Jamie did say,
'Away with this foolish mome!
He shall be hanged, and the other burned,
So soone as I come home'.

At Flodden Field the Scots come in,
Which made our Englishmen faine;
At Bramstone Greene this battaile was seene,
There was king Jamie slain.

Then presently the Scots did flie,
Their cannons they left behind;
Their ensignes gay were won all away,
Our souldiers did beate them blinde.

To tell you plaine, twelve thousand were slaine
That to the fight did stand,
And many prisoners tooke that day,
The best in all Scotland.

That day made many a fatherlesse child,
And many a widow poore,
And many a Scottish gay lady
Sate weeping in her bower.

Jack with a feather was all lapt in leather,
His boastings were all in vaine;
He had such a chance, with a new morrice-dance,
He never went home againe.

The Souters of Selkirk

Up wi' the souters of Selkirk
And doun wi' the Earl of Home;
And up wi' a' the braw lads
That sew the single-soled shoon.

Fye upon yellow and yellow,
And fye upon yellow and green,
But up wi' the true blue and scarlet
And up wi' the single-soled sheen.

Up wi' the souters of Selkirk,
For they are baith trusty and leal;
And up wi' the men o' the Forest,
And doun wi' the Merse to the deil.

Extract from Selkirk after Flodden
(a widow's dirge, October 1513)

It's but a month the morn
Sin' a' was peace and plenty;
Oor hairst was halflins shorn,
Eident men and lasses denty.
But noo it's a' distress-
Never mair a merry meeting';
For half the bairns are faitherless,
And a' the women greetin'.
    O Flodden Field!

Miles and miles round Selkirk toun,
Where forest flow'rs are fairest,
Ilka lassie's stricken doun,
Wi' fate that fa's the sairest.
A' the lads they used to meet
By Ettrick braes or Yarrow
Lyin' thrammelt head and feet
In Brankstone's deadly barrow!
    O Flodden Field!

Frae every cleuch and clan
The best o' the braid Border
Rose like a single man
To meet the royal order.
Oor Burgh toun itsel'
Sent seventy doun the glen;
Ask Fletcher how they fell,
Bravely fechtin', ane to ten!
    O Flodden Field!

Round about their gallant king,
For country and for croun,
Stude the dauntless Border ring,
Till the last was hackit doun.
I blame na what has been-
They maun fa' that canna flee-
But oh, to see what I hae seen
To see what now I see!
    O Flodden Field!

Extract from Edinburgh after Flodden

Right bitter was the agony, that wrung that soldier proud,
Thrice did he strive to answer, and thrice he groaned aloud.
Then he gave the riven banner, to the old man's shaking hand,
Saying - "that is all I bring ye from the bravest in the land!
Ay! Ye may look upon it - it was guarded well and long,
By your brothers and your children, by the valliant and tyhe strong.
One by one they fell around it, as the archers laid them low,
Grimly dying, still unconquered, with their faces to the foe.
Ay! Ye may well look upon it - there is more than honour there,
Else be sure, I had not brought it, from the field of dark despair.
Never yet was royal banner, steeped in such a costly dye,
It hath lain upon a bosom, where no other shroud shall lie.
Sirs! I charge you, keep it holy, keep it as a sacred thing,
For the stain ye see upon it, was the life blood of your King!"

Woe and woe and lamentation, what a piteous cry was there!
Widows, maidens, mothers, children, shrieking, sobbing in despair.
Through the streets the death word rushes, spreading terro, sweeping on.
"Jesu Christ! Our King hath fallen - O Great God, King James is gone!
Holy mother Mary, shield us, Thou who erst did lose thy son!
O the blackest day for Scotland that she ever knew before!
O our King- the good, the noble, shall we see him never more?
Woe to us and woe to Scotland, O our sons, our sons and our men!
Surely some have 'scaped the Southron, surely some will come again!

"All so thick they lay together, When the stars lit up the sky,
That I knew not who were stricken, or who yet remained to die."

"If our King be taken from us, we are left to guard his son,
Up! And haste ye through the city, stir the burghers stout and true!
Gather all our scattered people, Fling the banner out once more -
Randolph Murray! do though bear it, As it erst was borne before;
Never Scottish heart will leave it, when they see their monarch's gore!"

Extract from Flodden Field

After these lords were fallen and fled, and companies left captainless;
Being sore 'stonisht in that stead, did fall to flight both mor or less;
Whom Stanley with his total strength, pursued right sore down the plain;
Where on the King he light at length, which fighting was with all his main.

When his approach the King percieved, with stomach stout he him withstood;
His Scots right bravely them behaved, and boldly there the battle bode.
But when the English arrows shot, on each part did so pierce and gall,
That ere they came to handy strokes, a number great on ground did fall.

The King himself was wounded sore, an arrow fierce in's forehead light,
That hardly he could fight any more, the blood so blemished his sight.
Yet like a warrier stout he stayed, and fiercely did exort that tide,
His men to be nothing dismayed, but battle boldly there to bide.

"Fight on, my men," the King then said, "yet fortune she may turn the scale;
And for my wounds be not dismayed, nor ever let your courage fail."
Thus dying, did he brave appear, till shades of death did close his eyes;
Till then he did his soldiers chear, and raise their courage to the skiea.

But what availed his valour great, or bold device? All was but in vain,
His captains keen failed at his feet, and standard bearer down was slain;
The Archbishop of St Andrews brave, King james his son in base begot,
That doleful day did death receive, with many a lusty lord-like Scot.

As the Earl of Catness and Castel, Morton and Fair for all their power,
The Earl of Arell and Athell, Lord Maxwell with his brethren four;
And last of all among to lave, King James himself to death was brought,
Yet by whose fact few could perceive, but Stanley still most like was thought.

After the king and captains slain, the commons straight did fall to flight,
The Englishmen pursued amain, and never ceased while sun gave light;
Then the Earl of Surrey made to sound, a trumpet to retreat anon,
And captains caused to keep their ground, till morrow next while night was done.

But the English soldiers all that night, although weary were with toil,
The Scotchmen costly slain in fight, of jewels rich spared not to spoil;
The corpse of many worthy wight, they uncased of his comely array,
And many a baron brave and knight, their bodies there all naked lay.

Back Cover: King James IV's Sword. Illustration by Michelle Payne.